PRACTICAL GUIDES

MUSIC

TEACHING WITHIN THE
NATIONAL CURRICULUM

BARRY BARKER

Published by Scholastic Publications Ltd,
Villiers House, Clarendon Avenue,
Leamington Spa, Warwickshire CV32 5PR

© 1992 Scholastic Publications Ltd.

Written by Barry Barker
Edited by Christine Lee
Sub-edited by Christine Firth
Designed by Sue Limb
Illustrated by Janet Wickham
Photographs by Peter Corbett (pp 5, 7, 11, 19, 27, 35, 43, 51, 55, 65, 73, 79, 87, 93, 107, 115, 137 and 155), Richard Butchins (p 101), Bob Bray (p 123) and Mike Turner (p 145)

Printed by Ebenezer Baylis, Worcester

Front cover designed by Sue Limb
Front cover illustrated by Peter Brown (Maggie Mundy agency)

British Library Cataloguing in Publication Data

A catalogue record for this book is available from the British Library.

ISBN 0-590-53012-7

Contents

Introduction

Music in the curriculum

In 1982 the Gulbenkian Foundation published a report entitled *The Arts in Schools* in which the argument for including the arts in the school curriculum was cogently set out. The report sees the arts as making a vital contribution to the process of the development of human intelligence, the ability for creative thought and action and of feeling and sensibility. In addition, it speaks of the exploration of values, the understanding of cultural change and the development of physical and perceptual skill, and argues strongly against the idea that the arts are some kind of educational decoration of value only to the less academically gifted.

The Gulbenkian Report is one of the most convincing of documents which argue for the inclusion of the arts in school. It is probable that music, of all the art forms, is most in need of champions, occupying, as it often seems, the Cinderella status among curriculum subjects. In his foreward to Margaret Hope-Brown's book, *Music with Everything* (Frederick Warne, 1973), D.E. Pennington wrote:

'There seems to be general agreement that what we want for our children is a fuller, richer life. Music helps to develop a finer aesthetic sense; it offers a chance to participate in something active, creative and joyful. The emotional development of children seems particularly heightened when music has its place in integrated learning.'

Music facilities and practice in a school can be enhanced or diminished by the arrival or departure of a single member of staff who is wholly depended upon. Unless all general class teachers learn to accept music as part of their general curriculum, and understand the importance of their role, it is likely that this situation will continue to be common.

Music in the National Curriculum

The importance of music to the overall education and well-being of our pupils is now well established with the introduction of a National Curriculum for music. Although the appearance of the National Curriculum document, *Music in the National Curriculum*, will not greatly change the ways in which some schools have been accustomed to teaching the subject, many teachers are worried that they lack the proper training. Despite the fact that the document has been written with good existing practice in mind, teachers are worried that while the attainment targets are clear enough, the formulation and development of the processes and activities needed to reach these targets will make heavy demands upon staff who are already heavily committed.

It is hoped that this book will provide the general class teacher with a broad scheme of possibilities which will be found useful, in terms of National Curriculum requirements, in the working classroom.

Far too many teachers think that they are not 'musical' and are therefore unwilling to try activities for which others, as they see it, have a natural talent. It is these same teachers who, having successfully taught maths, English, geography and history for years, but without a degree in any of these subjects, balk at music because they see it as a gift, obtainable only by accident. A great many number of people do, in fact, have that 'gift', many more than would own up to a gift in mathematics.

After all, if music is available to all children, then why should it not be so to all teachers? The means by which all primary teachers can run effective music lessons have been gathered together in these pages. All the approaches set out here have been used in the 'generalist' classroom. No demand that teachers should be able to play the piano is made, and ways in which the requirements of the National Curriculum can be met are described without assuming previous musical knowledge. It is hoped that, while using approaches which contain 'musical knowledge', teachers who claim to 'know nothing about music' will become more confident and make musical discoveries along with their children. However, it is also hoped that school music co-ordinators will find value in these pages.

The first half of the book deals with the skills and activities specifically prescribed by the National Curriculum for performing and composing (Attainment Target 1) and listening and appraising (Attainment Target 2) at Key Stages One and Two. Ideas for approaches to assessment are also outlined. This is followed by chapters of a more general nature which discuss a number of topics such as the use of guitar chords, the recorder, orchestral instruments, electronic equipment and ethnic music. Chapter 20 provides a dip-in collection of practical music activities that support the ideas presented. This is followed by an invaluable annotated list of available printed resources that will help teachers choose publications suitable to their level of musical skill. The book concludes with a handy glossary of terms.

An attempt has been made to make this book 'friendly'. There is nothing in its pages which has not been successfully used in the classroom, and many activities have been modified by children themselves; there are no theories which have not been thoroughly tested by practical experience, but neither are there any activities which work without impetus from a lively teacher.

Among many good reasons for including music in the school curriculum is the possibility of the introduction of something creative, joyful and available to all.

Chapter 1
Key stage one

The need to define the attainment targets through clear and concise end of key stage statements will probably have raised in the minds of generalist classroom teachers the question, 'But what shall we need to do week by week?'

The programmes of study contain more detail but some teachers may still wonder if a generalist without specialist knowledge can enable pupils, for instance, to 'develop the technical skills needed to control the sounds of a range of tuned and untuned instruments, through playing simple pieces and accompaniments' [KS1, AT1, PoS (iv)].

It is hoped that, having read the introduction, the reader will have begun to feel happier about taking on the week by week music in her class, but this chapter will try to show how easily-managed activities can lead to the 'end of key stage statements' which will then seem realistically attainable and less imposing.

Attainment target 1: Performing and composing

End of key stage statement 1

Pupils should be able to 'Perform simple rhythmic and melodic patterns by ear and from symbols.'

To meet the needs of this end of key stage statement the teacher will need to build up discriminating listening by the children and their ability to echo the examples which she has played and sung to them. In order to do this the children will not only have to learn to listen carefully but to manage voices and those limbs with which rhythms will be played. Most of what is required can be found in Chapters 2 to 5 which deal specifically with these matters. The ability to recall melodies is something which comes with practice, providing also that the ability to sing in tune has been attained. This, too, is discussed in Chapter 5.

Performance 'from symbols' would imply that the children are required to read from standard notation, both rhythmic and pitched. However, the document is careful, at later key stages, to speak of 'notations' and at Key Stage One it is clear that it is some kind of non-standard notation which is suggested. There is a body of opinion, supported by printed resources, which suggests that rhythmic standard notation (minims, crotchets, quavers and so on) *can* be used at this very early stage. This is likely to be rarely seen in Key Stage One classes, except when the recorder is used, and the symbols are more likely to be objects, pictures (Chapter 4, page 34, Figure 3), cereal packets and even children whose names provide the word rhythms (see Chapter 20, page 156, 'Name rhythms').

These and the repeated rhythms of words or phrases from songs and rhymes (see Chapter 4, page 29) provide plenty of accessible material. Additionally there are rhythm grids (see Chapter 20, page 167) which can either be provided by the teacher or, with experience, children can design for themselves.

End of key stage statement 2

Pupils should be able to 'Sing in a group and play simple instruments, demonstrating some control of the sounds made.'

It is clear that the first experiences of singing will be by repeated phrases and little songs learned by rote. Many of the methods of symbolic notation of rhythmic patterns given in Chapter 4 will be useful in providing instrumental accompaniment to songs and Chapter 15 explains how chordal accompaniments, which have frequently been used with success in the reception year, can be employed.

Firstly, however, children will need to take part in the activities which provide experience of the sounds which instruments will produce; some of these appear in Chapter 6 and are also intended to help children discover sounds which can be available for composition. There is a section in Chapter 4 which deals with the introduction of instruments and both these chapters include ideas about how children's aptitude in the control of instrumental sounds can be developed. Chapter 9 gives advice about improving the quality of singing and breathing while Chapter 12 deals with performance and music sharing.

End of key stage statement 3

Pupils should be able to 'Investigate, choose and combine sounds to produce simple compositions.'

During the process of encouraging listening, sounds from the environment, from objects in the classroom and from a variety of instruments will have been considered (for example, see Chapter 6, page 45, 'Simple sound pictures').

Having established that these sounds exist, it is logical to assemble and use them for purposes similar to that of making collages in art lessons. Pictures, dramatic sequences and stories can be translated into, or accompanied by, thoughts expressed in the medium of sound. A short section in Chapter 2 (page 14) discusses story accompaniments and the story in Chapter 20 (page 169), which children named 'A giant came', is an example of material which can be used at story-time, discussed through music and then retold in the form of a composition.

Rhythms and effects can be improvised to accompany songs and rhymes using a variety of sound sources, including voices, and small groups can make up happy, sad, angry music as a group might work on a frieze.

As a prelude to the making of melodies for songs, two or three chime bars can be used to make music for children's names. Providing these are chosen at a suitable pitch children can play their own names which can then be repeated a number of times by the group, thus providing further practice in singing simple melodic patterns.

End of key stage statement 4

Pupils should be able to **'Record their own compositions and communicate them to others.'**

It is desirable that small children learn to use a simple cassette recorder since this is useful in a variety of language activities. This method of recording pieces requires little explanation, but graphic scores of the simplest kind can also be written. When children have decided how they think sounds can be represented on paper, a score can be made. The effectiveness of the score can be tested when, at a later date, an attempt to recreate the first performance is tried.

In the process of inventing notations, children will discover what works and what is less effective and in time will produce scores which are not only pleasingly specific but attractive to look at. In all playing activities, the two duties of performance need to be kept in mind: the duty of the performers to communicate with their audience and that of the audience – to listen!

Attainment target 2: Listening and appraising

End of key stage statement 1

Pupils should be able to **'Listen attentively and respond to short pieces of music from different times and cultures and in different styles, showing an awareness of differences and similarities.'**

Chapters 2 and 3 and a section of Chapter 20 contain many activities which encourage children to listen attentively and with understanding. In Chapter 3 there is also an argument, supported by research, which strongly suggests that to encourage children to be aurally aware has beneficial effects on their performance across the curriculum. It is therefore clear that the kind of listening activities described in these chapters leads directly to a more effective approach to the process of listening to music.

To make the actual introduction of a piece of music a central part of a lesson is likely to be successful with only a proportion of the class, but if the music can be included as an activity related to another part of the curriculum, then the music can become familiar to the children before it is actually discussed. It may be that music of a certain style is used in a movement lesson and that in a topic-related art lesson a further playing helps to remind the class of the experiences and discussions that have already taken place. Now, when the music is familiar, the music can become the centre of discussion in a situation similar to story-time, and the ways in which it achieves its effect and the devices employed by the composer can be discussed.

If there is an historical element then the story-time set-up lends itself to description, with pictures and perhaps objects, of life and people of the time at which the composer lived. The life of the composer himself may seem less relevant to children than the way of life of children like themselves. The historical setting in social terms is much more important at this stage than the place of the piece in the history of music.

End of key stage statement 2

Pupils should be able to **'Talk, in simple terms, about sounds and music they have listened to, performed or composed.'**

It should not be difficult to satisfy this requirement. Every lesson is, in some respect, a language lesson and if children are constantly encouraged to discuss and to evaluate their discoveries and to use descriptive language and to learn conventional terms, then the attainment of a musical vocabulary holds no more mysteries than the general area of language development across the curriculum.

Chapter 2
Getting started

The day that the new reception class assembles in a classroom and bids farewell to nervous mums and dads is, as teachers well know, the beginning of a voyage of discovery – not only for the children but for the teacher as well.

Although the teacher may have met most of the children before and will, no doubt, have talked to parents, to the children themselves and perhaps to nursery teachers, this may not guarantee the real pre-knowledge of the children which could be of much help in the process which is about to start. Their environment is new, their reactions to their teacher will be varied and the interactions between children in the group may reveal quite new behaviour. Some will not yet see themselves as part of the group, but will seek the old one-to-one relationship. Some will need to learn to share while others, already experienced in the hard school of personal survival techniques, will grab everything attractive in sight and probably attempt to take it home.

The first task may well be to show the children that they are part of a group and to establish routines by which they can be moved round the school safely. Even before this, you may need to establish that you are there to be listened to as well as to listen and to lay down some kind of appropriate routine from the outset.

Soon, however, you will begin to discover the things required to form a basis for teaching. For example, it may emerge that one child has a vivid imagination while another has poor motor skills. In this process of discovery, learning needs will be identified, some of which can be satisfied, either entirely or in part, by musical activities. In this chapter we shall look at some common reception class needs and suggest ways in which the use of music can play a part in their satisfaction.

Listening and fine body control

It is often remarked that although most children can *see* perfectly, many may not yet have learned to *look*. For example, a class of infants took shoe boxes into the playground and collected leaf mould during a project on mini-beasts. When they returned, they searched the black stuff for animals and, among the seven or eight kinds visible to the naked eye, there were a number of violet garden beetles. When asked to draw what they had found, a number of children drew what can only be described as 'beetle-drive' beetles. They had failed to look.

A parallel can be drawn with hearing and listening; although most children's hearing is unimpaired, listening with discrimination is undoubtedly a skill that has to be learned. Similarly, the ability to manage one's body with increasingly finer control is also a skill which has to be developed.

It is in the development of these two skills in particular – listening and fine body control – that music can play an important role, and in which lies the key to success in so many areas of the curriculum.

The child who is not encouraged to listen to and imitate words in early life will not, later on, be ready to make sentences. In such a case, his ability to communicate will be limited until the skill is acquired. The opportunity to discover and discriminate between different sound qualities and to think of ways in which they can be used in communication will widen a child's vision and stimulate his imagination. From this follows the actual production of sound through physical means, either instrumentally or vocally, which will require practice and encouragement and, in some cases, discovery.

Co-operation within a group will be necessary if activities are to be successful. The very nature of such group work encourages self-control as well as control of an instrument or the voice.

Early listening activities

Our world is full of elements which discourage the sensitive use of our ears. A successor to the radio programme *Children's Hour* is now being broadcast because it was realised that the use of the ear as the receptor of stimulation and interest was fading. This programme is not aimed simply at the very young but encourages all children to rediscover the skill of listening.

Listening needs to become a part of life from the outset. Some people believe that listening activities cannot be 'music', because they consider that listening activities are not 'creative'. However, creativity is undoubtedly served by sharpened aural perception, as well as skilful hands and voice. Moreover, it is likely that the children will enjoy more of what they produce if they are competent in such skills.

It is by the inclusion of the kind of activities which follow that the ability to listen attentively will be built up. Careful use of the ear will lead to the ability to memorise and internalise musical patterns and songs and will help to develop a discriminating approach to sounds which will, in turn, demand refinement of playing skills (AT2).

Each day make a point of inconspicuously including listening activities. Any of the following ideas can be used for introducing listening skills.

Dropping a pin

KS1, AT2 (a), PoS (ii).
Before introducing a new activity, gather the children together and encourage a hushed atmosphere. Hold a pin inside a cardboard box so that the children cannot see what you are doing and ask the children to put up their hands when they hear the pin drop. Wait for complete silence, then drop the pin.

Discuss the result in a quiet voice, then introduce the chosen activity. Question the children as to what the instruction was, maintaining the hushed atmosphere, and then tell them to comply with the instruction.

Box of objects

KS1, AT2 (a), PoS (i) and (ii).
Fill a small box with a number of objects. Shake it. Question the children about the likely contents. How many objects are in the box – one, a few or many?

Shaky pots

KS1, AT2 (a), PoS (ii).
Make two sets of 'shaky pots' using photographer's film containers. Any camera shop will be happy to give you as many as you require, so ask if you might leave a box in the shop to collect the empty containers as films are brought in for processing.

Divide the pots into pairs and put similar items into each pair so that the pots sound the same when shaken but are different from the sounds made by other pots. Let each child have one pot, then ask them to find a partner with a pot which sounds the same as theirs.

Chime bar

KS1, AT2 (a), PoS (i).
See how long the note of a chime bar can be heard. Make the note short or long by damping the bar with a finger. Using a soft voice, question the children about the note. Was it long or short? Was it high or low? Don't forget that long, short, low and high are comparative terms and, for that matter, they are conventional rather than descriptive terms.

Story-time

Incorporate sounds into the daily story. Invent or modify stories so that characters can easily be identified by sounds. For example:
• the bells of three reindeer could be different;
• the Billy Goats Gruff could make different sounds with their hooves;
• three railway engines could make different puffing sounds.

Body control activities

Children need to become aware of what their bodies can do and how they can initiate and manage movement with increasingly finer control. Such movement includes not only that of the limbs but also that of the vocal cords and breath.

Handling and controlling instruments, which includes keeping them quiet when not required, also needs to be practised. Activities which help children to discover how an instrument makes its sounds and how many different sounds it can make, as well as fine motor skill games like the Tambourine Race described below, are valuable as the children prepare to make their own music.

Story accompaniments

KS1, AT1 (b), (c) and (d), PoS (iv) to (x).
Sounds which illustrate and enhance parts of a story need not necessarily be made on instruments but can be produced using hands, feet, knee-slapping, vocal sounds and the many ways of using indrawn and exhaled breath.

Let the children take turns at providing accompaniments for an appropriate story using these sounds. Encourage the children to increase or decrease the volume of the sounds made in response to the movements of your hand. For example, encourage them to make loud sounds when you hold your hand up high, descending in volume until a really soft sound is reached as you lower your hand. Concentrate on getting them to experiment vocally and with other parts of the body and to respond quickly to changes in dynamics. The ability to reduce a loud noise will be particularly useful!

Tambourine race

KS1, AT1, PoS (iv).
The Tambourine Race involves two equal teams of children seeing which one can pass a tambourine most quickly from one end of a line to the other. The difficulty lies in the fact that this must be done without the tambourines making a sound. If a sound

is made, the tambourine must go back two spaces. Thus the handling of the instrument must be controlled with great precision and the children are encouraged to develop the ability to make sure that an instrument makes its sound only when required.

The dragon's gold

KS1, AT2 (a), PoS (ii).
The production of planned sounds can be used at story-time. In longer music sessions, play The Dragon's Gold and make up a story about a dragon's treasure for similar treatment.

The Dragon's Gold is a game in which a child, representing the dragon, stands blindfolded astride a miscellaneous pile of classroom instruments, representing the treasure. Choose children to take turns to creep up from various directions and try to steal a piece of the treasure without the dragon hearing them. If the dragon hears a sound and can point to the thief, the child will become the next dragon.

Hidden instruments

KS1, AT2 (a), PoS (i).
Games like Hidden Instruments, as well as being useful for developing the ability to handle instruments, will also promote listening and memory skills.

Hidden Instruments involves playing a musical instrument chosen from a number behind a screen. Ask the children to try to guess which instrument was played. When a child thinks she knows the answer, let her go behind the screen, play the appropriate instrument, then choose another to play. The next child must play both and then add one, and so on. This game, or variations on it, can be played throughout the primary age range.

For the sake of hygiene, Hidden Instruments should not be played with instruments that need to be played with the mouth.

Singing from day one

'Pupils should memorise and internalise short musical patterns and simple songs, and imitate and recall simple rhythms and melodies' [KS1, AT1, PoS (i)].

There was a time when music in school was synonymous with 'singing'. Although there was some 'percussion band work', with the possible use of tonic sol-fa notation, singing was the main musical experience. The advances in school music, while excellent in most respects, have somehow caused class singing to be thought of as a feature of 'the olden days'.

Children should be encouraged to sing together from day one and, with suitable material and approaches as described in Chapter 5, there is no reason why this thoroughly sociable and enjoyable activity should not be a constant feature of primary school life.

Songs for reception year children

Finger rhymes and counting songs are perfect starting material. Many teachers will be familiar with *This Little Puffin* which contains many pre-school and reception year songs. These should be sung as a social activity between teacher and children. The 'let's sing together' feeling needs to be established rather than the teacher playing the piano and either towering above or remaining outside the singing.

Pitch and clarity

Care needs to be taken not to use too high a pitch. What is pleasantly comfortable for the teacher will usually be suitable for the children. However, teachers with naturally good voices sometimes forget that, when first starting to sing, young children's voices need to be pitched at the level at which they speak; it is only after practice that higher notes can be accurately placed. This is particularly important for children who have had little or no experience in singing.

Setting an example by singing the words clearly, sometimes appearing to 'over-do' the use of lips and tongue, is most important. At this age children will imitate an example and not think it odd to emphasise the vowels and consonants. There is often little need to do more than to draw their attention to the desirability of clearly heard words.

Singing games

Singing games such as 'Five little buns in a baker's shop' can be sung while the children act out the words and, incidentally, practise simple subtraction. Such games should take place on the carpet in the corner of the classroom rather than in a large space like the hall. It can be intimidating to have to send one's voice into a large space, whereas the informal story-time atmosphere is a good one in which to build confidence and, also, one in which the teacher can hear who can sing and who needs help.

Enjoying singing

Finally, it is important to treat singing as an important and pleasant activity. Once a teacher shows some kind of negative attitude, the children will begin to question the validity of the activity and the less able may give up. It is partly for this reason that, when planning an assembly or performance, there should be no selection on the grounds of 'this child can sing but that one cannot'. Given time, encouragement and the opportunity to sing suitable material, the vast majority of children will happily join in.

It is in this early performing situation that it is most important for the children to know the song really well. The meagre wailing of a group is painful enough for the audience, but the singers will be quick to feel that they are making fools of

themselves and will, on future occasions, be difficult to motivate. On the other hand, the benefits of a lusty performance will work wonders for singing morale.

Making use of the cassette recorder

The cassette recorder is in common use in the infant classroom to give children, either individually or in small groups, the opportunity to listen to stories, to record their own stories, to record their own performances, and so on. For any of these uses it is necessary for the children to learn to operate the machine which, as time goes on, will prove to be a useful skill. It is good for children to discover just what the cassette recorder can do.

Recording the class activities

Make a recording of the children without their knowledge and play it back to them. This will not only produce an excellent language session but also introduce the recorder as an interesting listening tool, leading to language and drama. 'What were we doing?' or 'Who was speaking?' are questions which will provide concentrated listening and careful thought.

Encourage the children to devise sounds to represent parts of a story, such as using a glockenspiel to represent a stream. Then record the sounds and play them back to the children. This provides the 'performance element' which encourages commitment and self-discipline and starts the children on the path to self-evaluation.

Evaluation activities

The use of the cassette recorder, either by children themselves in their groups or by the teacher during the performance stage, will provide an added opportunity to evaluate work done. It is not always possible to do full justice to a piece at one listening, but with the use of a recording a number of aspects, such as mood, effectiveness of performance and so on, can be considered singly at each repeated playing.

'How could we make it better?' is a simple question which encourages understanding of evaluation and develops the necessary vocabulary. If you ever feel at a loss as to how to discuss the merits of a piece, there need be no more difficulty than when faced with a paint-soaked piece of sugar paper. For example, you could ask, 'Would you like to tell us about it?' or 'Is that how you meant it, or do you want to change it?' Similarly, if children have chosen to use musical instruments to illustrate moments from a story, the evaluation process could be directed as follows:

'Let's listen to see if we can guess what is happening in the music. Were we right? Why did you think it was the snake? What did John do to make it like the movements of a snake?'

The opportunity to respect each other's work and to take turns in discussion and, sometimes, to bear criticism gives practice in true life skills.

Discussion and deduction activities

A session with a tape recorder can be followed usefully by discussion and deduction activities. Record a simple and readily recognisable sound, but remember that for the children merely to identify it is a poor use of the material. If a supermarket checkout is recorded, for example, encourage the children to consider how many items were bought and whether the 'right money' was paid or change given. Was it possible to tell whether it was a man or a woman on the till?

Consider the sound of someone washing up. Can you tell how many had dinner? Did

they have anything to drink? Did they have something which was eaten with the fingers or were there knives and forks involved? Only one? If it was a knife, what might they have been eating?

Self-expression activities

The tape recorder not only is useful in these ways but also can encourage clear speech and confident self-expression. Children quickly learn how to conduct interviews or record their thoughts on to tape. If sensible routines for its use are developed, there is no reason why the tape recorder should not be operated by the children themselves.

Conclusion

All the skills mentioned in this chapter, although appropriate for development in the reception year, may be found to be undeveloped in some older children and that is why the chapter is called 'Getting started'. It may be that the 'starter' activities suggested need to be used not only in the reception year but also in later years of the infant school and even in Y3. The next four chapters deal with specific areas of work in the infant age range, but obviously some older children will also need to experience starter activities. The approach will be somewhat different but the fundamental needs will be the same.

Chapter 3
Developing listening skills

'The development of the ability to listen to and appraise music, including knowledge of musical history, our diverse musical heritage, and a variety of other musical traditions.' (AT2)

Developing discriminating listening

If children are to use and appreciate music as an alternative language with which to express thoughts and feelings, they must build on the basic skills. The most fundamental of these is listening.

Fortunately, it is relatively seldom that a teacher has a pupil with a hearing disability. Yet one often comes across the complaint from teachers that children do not listen. The ear is one of the five sensors through which an individual will learn. Failure to use it with discrimination is a serious drawback in the process of education. The *raison d'etre* for the improvement of listening skills is, therefore, clearly one of general child development.

In all its forms, music is clearly dependent upon listening. A conductor, an orchestral player or a singer cannot succeed without being a good listener, and a composer must learn to listen so efficiently that his imagination can reverse the process and enable him to set down music heard only in his head. In the process of musical education, the sense of listening is sharpened and refined. The benefits of this refinement do more than further musical prowess. The development of listening skills is valuable across the whole school curriculum. Not only does it enhance the potential for enjoying music, but also it opens up a facility for the reception of much more general information and experience.

It may be that some teachers would see the practical advantages of music across the curriculum as more important than its aesthetic considerations, but because of its obvious dependence upon listening skills, music is an ideal vehicle to either end. Music is one means of developing skills towards more effective progress across the curriculum, but it is also important to see improved listening skills as a path to the development of music as a creative art and as a method of communication and of self-expression. It is undoubtedly true that general musical activities contribute to the improvement of listening skills. But the encouragement of discriminating listening needs to be an aim and not just a by-product. It is for this reason that specifically designed listening activities need to be included in classroom musical activities.

Declining listening abilities?

When the Bullock Report stated that children's listening ability appeared not to have diminished over time, a number of primary class teachers in Worcestershire voiced misgivings at the findings. In their view primary children's listening performance *had* become less effective and an investigation was mounted to see if there was cause for concern and what action might need to be taken. The details of the research and its conclusions were published in *The Music Teacher*, October 1985.

Teachers' questionnaire

A questionnaire was circulated in the Hereford and Worcester, Sandwell and Birmingham Education Authorities and was completed by 60 primary teachers who had five years' experience or more. The questionnaire sought to establish a starting point from which remedial material might be developed. The results were as follows:

Q. Do you think that listening ability is in decline?
75 per cent replied YES.
25 per cent replied NO.
Many among the 25 per cent pointed out that the difference between ability and actual performance needed to be made clear. They thought that the ability had not lessened although they agreed that actual listening performance was less satisfactory.

Q. If you have observed a decline in listening performance, what factors do you consider contribute to it?
30 per cent replied: lack of conversation with young children at home through:
• both parents working;
• parental attitudes;
• television used as dummy;
• younger parents and homes less settled.
60 per cent replied: we live in an increasingly noisy world; a shut-off mechanism is developed so that children exclude important and unimportant sounds alike.
10 per cent replied: little listening practice is given without the help of visual aids.

Q. In what ways have you observed listening failure in school?
40 per cent replied: poor response to verbal instructions.
10 per cent replied: poor oral comprehension work.
20 per cent replied: difficulty in distinguishing both sounds and pitches.
25 per cent replied: failure in reading activities.
5 per cent replied: failure in rhythmic imitation games.

Q. What activities are used to try to remedy poor listening skills?

33 per cent replied: verbal response to memory tests.

24 per cent replied: rhythmic work.

16 per cent replied: verbal comprehension.

12 per cent replied: sound identification.

As may be seen, by far the most striking evidence of poor skill was observed in response to the spoken word. The greatest cause, however, was thought to be environmental problems and not the lack of language in the early years. It seemed, on the whole, that the symptoms were being treated rather than the 'disease', the seeming lack of skill to discriminate.

Designing a test

As response to the spoken word seemed a significant failing, it was decided to design a test which would measure improvement in this activity. The tests would be aimed initially at young children and take place at the beginning and the end of a term. During the term, specially prepared teaching material would be used which would be directed at the problem as identified. Control schools would administer the tests but not use the teaching material, and it would then be possible to see whether work in sound discrimination would enhance general listening performance. The teaching material would involve sound sorting, sound memory, rhythmic discrimination, sound awareness and composition at an appropriate level, but the tests would take the form of spoken instructions on tape which required a pencil and paper response. There would be no numbering of questions, as this might confuse young children, and a set amount of preparation involving vocabulary and pictures to be used in the test would be provided for.

A typical extract from the test is as follows: 'Next, you can see the picture of a bird and beside it is a cat, a cup of tea, a clock and a gate. Draw a line under the cat.'

Using the test

When a pilot run of the test had been made and necessary modifications to the testing procedure as well as agreed flexibilities in marking established, a short training programme was mounted for the participating teachers. This included a video of a class actually using the teaching materials. Volunteers were called to administer the test at each end of the project term but not actually to introduce the teaching materials. These teachers would act as controls and continue their customary teaching programme.

Result of the test

When the results were collated and assessed it was found that the control classes showed an improvement of five per cent in the end of term test. Those classes which had been made aware of the need to listen carefully showed an average improvement of 26 per cent.

Listening activities used in the suggested programme

The following activities are examples of the sorts of activities used to enhance listening performance in the investigation cited above. They are recognised as sound and effective in their purpose and offer the non-specialist teacher ideas for adapting to her own classroom situation.

Several sounds from one instrument

KS1, AT2 (a), PoS (ii).
KS1, AT2 (b), PoS (iv).
For this game you will need a musical instrument (the tambourine is especially good).

Get the children to sit in a circle. Give one child the chosen instrument and ask her to play it before passing it to her

neighbour who should try to play a different sound. Explain that the point of the game is to see how far the instrument can travel before someone repeats a sound. When a sound is repeated, start the game again from scratch with the next child.

The ideas heard in the first run are used and often developed by those playing after restarting the game. This game not only is an excellent listening activity but also encourages memory and knowledge of instruments and other sound sources.

The sound tins

KS1, AT2 (a), PoS (i) and (ii).
Collect together the following: twelve metal tins with lids (such as mustard or golden syrup tins), gloss paint in white, red, yellow, green, blue, orange and pink, a range of small items, such as matches, dried peas, buttons, rice, paper-clips.

Paint six of the tin lids white and the rest red, yellow, green, blue, orange and pink respectively. It is important to use the same type of paint, as different kinds of paints can produce different resonances.

Arrange the tins in pairs – one white topped and one coloured – then fill each pair with small objects so that, when shaken, each tin will sound exactly the same as its partner.

Games with the tins can take many forms in both whole class situations and in groups. As a class discuss the possible contents. The nature of each sound will provide much language work and aural experience.
• Ask the children to sort them into similarly sounding pairs. Exchange the lids of the coloured tins from time to time to present a fresh challenge.
• Line up the tins in random pairs in the centre of a circle of children. Ask one child to 'play' a white tin and ask another to find the coloured tin whose sound matches it; only one try or 'guess' is allowed. As the game proceeds the children will begin to remember which tins are required to make pairs. Divide the children into two teams,

and encourage each team to try to 'capture' a pair. The team with the most pairs wins.
• Organise a timed sorting race between pairs of children. This could provide some very good mathematics work in the form of block graphs and league tables (see page 96). Let three teams compete each day; one before morning break, one before lunch and one in the afternoon.

Although this activity seems appropriate to the primary school, it was once used during aural skills sessions at a Conservatoire of Music and was proved to be far more valuable than might at first be thought.

Copying rhythms

KS1, AT1, PoS (i), (ii), (iv), (v) and (vii).
Clap a simple rhythm and ask the children to repeat it. In the following example, words are used to indicate the rhythm.
Teacher: (claps) Rice Krispies, Rice Krispies.
(The children repeat the rhythm by clapping.)
Teacher: (claps) Shredded Wheat, Shredded Wheat.

(The children repeat the rhythm by clapping).

This activity is of no value if a gap is left between the teacher's rhythm and the children's reply. Begin your next rhythm as soon as the children have finished theirs so that there is a steady flow. Nine or ten copyings of patterns is probably sufficient before developing the activity but this will depend upon how well the children do.

Having begun the activity with your hands in full view of the class, hide your hands behind some kind of screen and repeat the activity. This emphasises to the children that they must rely upon their ears rather than their eyes. This may seem to make the activity harder, but you will probably find that children perform with a sharper and more accurate response. Develop the activity further by clapping your hands on your knees as well as clapping your hands together. Once the children have to discriminate between the sounds of hand and knee, the activity becomes much harder and a slower pace needs to be taken. Depending upon the children's skill, the pace of clapping can be varied.

Peg Leg Pete

KS1, AT1, PoS (viii).
Ask four children to hide behind a screen, then let one of them knock as though outside a door. Encourage the rest of the class to call out, 'Who's that knocking at my door?'

Ask one of the children to disguise his voice and reply, 'It is me, Peg Leg Pete, come home from the sea.'

Ask the rest of the class to try to guess whose was the mystery voice. Let the child who gives the correct answer replace Peg Leg Pete and join the children behind the screen. Let them decide who is to go next by throwing a die or drawing lots from a bag.

Sherlock Ears

KS1, AT2 (a) and (b), PoS (ii).
The name of this activity was made up by some junior children who invented 'The Great Sound Detective' and drew his picture, substituting an ear trumpet for the usual magnifying glass.

Record a series of sounds on a cassette recorder so that a story or dramatic sequence is implied.

Let one child be the Great Sound Detective, Sherlock Ears, and listen to the story on earphones, or let the whole class play detective, and recount or record their version of the story in an appropriate manner.

Taking a tape recorder for a walk

KS1, AT2 (a) and (b), PoS (ii).
Allow a small group of children to take a tape recorder around the school, recording the various sounds that they hear.

Back in the classroom, play the tape to the rest of the class and ask them to try to identify the route that the group took. Encourage them to listen carefully to the sounds and to describe what they think is happening.

Follow this up by allowing groups of

children to take turns at acting a dramatic sequence involving sound effects but no dialogue behind the backs of the rest of the class. Ask the rest of the class to say what is happening.

The hot and cold game

KS1, AT2 (a), PoS (i) and (iii).
The name of this game comes from expressions such as 'You're getting warmer', which signifies that someone is getting nearer to the solution of a problem.

Ask one child to leave the room, while the others hide a small object, such as a toy car, somewhere in the room. Explain to the rest of the class that when the child comes back, they must sing a song and adjust the volume depending on how far he is from the 'treasure', that is, when he is 'cold' they should sing softly and when he is 'warm' they should sing more loudly.

This is not always successful as the children tend to over-react and thus only very loud and very soft singing might ensue. If this should happen, hide the object yourself in a location unknown to the class. Let one child look for the treasure while you direct the volume of singing with your hand. In this way it is possible to ensure much more variety of volume.

Another variation would be to use a tape recorder instead of singing. The music from a tape recorder can be varied in volume to indicate 'hotness' or the reverse. Furthermore, when operated by a child, it provides practice in sensitive use of the tape recorder's controls. It is advisable to establish the range of volume at the outset by a demonstration of what the recorder can do. Remember also that the sound of a small cassette machine does not carry very far and that for large spaces, a bigger loudspeaker will be needed.

Messages in tunes

KS1, AT2 (a), PoS (i).

Introduce the children to the idea that classroom routines can be signalled by the playing of simple melodies on a glockenspiel or piano. One school has 'stand up', 'sit down' and 'hands together' music which is played on the piano in assembly. This appears to produce a prompt reaction which seems to be made more eagerly than when simple spoken instructions are used. In a classroom of another school, the 'put away your work' tune was five descending notes: G F E D C.

When this had been played and the teacher had looked round to see if it had been done, a snatch of tune specific to a particular table was used to indicate which group was to leave the room first. The hush, as the instruction was awaited, was remarkable and the neatness with which the whole operation was managed had to do with the children's clear enjoyment.

Encourage the children to compose musical codes to be used for a variety of classroom situations.

Chapter 4
Physical skills

'The development of the ability to perform and compose music with understanding.' (AT1)

The control of body and instruments in performing

The improvement of physical skills sounds as if it is the province of physical education. It is, of course, but physical education includes the kind of skill that one admires so much in an accomplished player of a musical instrument – the fine motor skills and, as wind players will know, the control of that myriad of tiny muscles which enable us to smile and frown.

It is comforting to think, as we marvel at the muscular control of a concert pianist, that there was a time when he had difficulty in bringing a spoon of baby food into the vicinity of his mouth and that it is only through practice and experience that

he has achieved the skills he now possesses.

Before a child is ready to play even a simple instrument, she needs to have made some progress in the development of fine motor skills and to have acquired a sense of rhythm. She will have had to learn to be a somewhat discriminating listener so as to be able both to monitor her own playing and to learn by example from others.

Rhythmic skills

'By the end of key stage 1, pupils should be able to perform simple rhythmic and melodic patterns by ear and from symbols' [KS1, AT1, (a) and (b), PoS (i), (ii), (iv), (v), (vi) and (vii)].

By having the opportunity to clap a steady pulse, to walk with a measured tread, and to speak a rhythmic rhyme, thus experiencing steady rhythm with the whole body, the feeling for rhythmic steadiness becomes recognisable to the child. The copying of a pulse or a simple pattern with the feet is particularly valuable to children who do not manage their body weight smoothly. Strangely enough, it is not always the more bulky figures who seem to have this difficulty; in fact, large adults are often good at managing their weight and are able to dance with considerable skill. Children who move awkwardly come in all shapes and sizes and if not given the opportunity to improve, they can continue to move awkwardly into adulthood.

Having attained a sense of rhythm is all very well, but the ability to reproduce or to invent a rhythmic pattern is an additional skill. Clapping or playing an instrument often involves bringing two freely moving objects together at a critical moment but, for a young child, even bringing a beater down on to a fixed surface at a given moment can be difficult. The arm, after all, has to begin its motion before the sound is required and at the last moment the wrist has to make a slight adjustment so that the whole series of movements culminates in an accurately timed sound. The ability to use both hands and even fingers independently is a far cry from the early work which an inexperienced child needs to cover, but remember that the concert pianist must, at some time, have been at the stage when rhythmic awareness first became physical response. It is likely that many infant children will be at this stage and teachers will need to plan appropriate activities.

The ability to imitate

In the early stages of the development of a child's rhythmic skills which, one hopes, takes place in the reception year or in Y1, the ability to imitate is most important. If a clapped rhythm can be repeated accurately by children, it is clear that they are listening and that they have sufficient motor control to make an accurate response. At Y1 or reception stage some will be able to do this, but there will always be those who have great difficulty. Imitation needs to be taught so that it is

understood that the repeated action must be an exact copy of the original.

To establish this principle, 'do as I do' activities are useful. Touch your nose with both hands and ask the children to copy. An air of excitement can be generated so that immediate response is made by changing gestures rapidly, such as hands on head, palms facing the class, hands on shoulders, little fingers pointing forward. ('Who has got the wrong fingers? Be careful! Get it exactly right.') Check whether anyone is lagging behind.

'Say what I say' activities can follow. These are also ideal for developing discriminating listening. Start by saying the names of things in the classroom in a normal voice, and ask the children to copy you. Then use a high-pitched voice, or a particularly soft or loud tone. Are they exactly copying? Try pointing to the various items, and explain that if you point to a table but say 'chair', then the children must be silent, saying the name of the object only if it is correctly identified. Breathless excitement can be generated with every member of the class straining to listen in order to give an accurate response.

The next stage is to combine spoken word and clapped rhythm, using the rhythms of words. For instance, you might say, 'Weet-a-bix, Weet-a-bix', rhythm-clapping the words at the same time, then encouraging the children to repeat what they hear. If the response is ragged, repeat the exercise, and evaluate the response. Try different phrases, letting them follow one another in a rhythmic sequence so that the children can follow without hesitation when only the rhythms are clapped. However, remember that to vary the length of the phrase is to invite hesitation and the value of the activity – to develop a smooth rhythmic skill – will be lost.

When clapping a rhythm without speaking the words, it is helpful to use one of the little breakfast cereal rhythms twice: Sugar Puffs, Sugar Puffs. The children do not need to know that your rhymes are guided by words. They are quoted here to

Rhythmic speaking of a rhyme with an accompaniment of pulsed or patterned clapping can resemble a musical performance and is usually enjoyed by all. Although essentially an infant activity, it has often been found to be useful with junior school children. Junior children who have not yet grasped the concept of rhythm need to be given the chance to catch up, and often do. Apart from this, the fact that the activity is enjoyed by juniors is reason enough for its continued use.

Using a rhythmic rhyme

KS1, AT1 (a) and (b).

A steady rhythm in speaking a rhyme needs to be established:

Oliver Cromwell lay buried and dead,
He, haw, buried and dead.
There grew an old apple-tree over his
    head,
He, haw, over his head.
The apples are ripe and ready to fall,
He, haw, ready to fall.
There came an old woman to gather
    them all,
He, haw, gather them all.
Oliver rose and gave her a drop,
He, haw, gave her a drop,
Which made the old woman go
    hippity-hop,
He, haw, hippity-hop.

This rhyme can be taught simply by allowing the children to speak the 'He, haw' lines and speaking the rest yourself. This can then be developed by letting the children clap the rhythm of the words as they speak.

When the children can say the whole rhyme, assisted perhaps with cue cards (eg. a picture of Oliver's grave, an old apple tree), a continuous speaking of repeated words, such as 'Hippity-hop, Hippity-hop' can be undertaken by some of the class while the rest speak the whole rhyme; this 'ostinato' (repeated section) can then be spoken and clapped and finally just clapped.

When developing a sense of rhythm and the physical skill to use it, this progression

demonstrate the kind of rhythm which fits together with the children's response and produces an ongoing flow. Many teachers will not need the words, and others will soon be able to dispense with their private use. Look at your hands while clapping and then shift your gaze to the class, saying, 'You can tell when to clap because I shall look at you'. The conductor's most compelling tools are her eyes.

This activity as well as the listening activities described in Chapter 3, is valuable for gaining attention at odd moments of the day and to begin the quietening process before story-time. Children soon begin to read the teacher's body language and an activity can be set up to fill in the time before the bell goes.

Try using a chopping motion of the arm to indicate 'I am dividing the class in two', then clap the rhythm to one of the groups. In this way a healthy competition can ensue to see who can most accurately repeat the rhythms.

of speak, speak and clap, clap is most useful. The spoken rhythm communicates itself to the hands. If instruments are given to children after having clapped successfully, it is advisable to reintroduce the speaking of the rhythm, as the steadying influence on an internally felt rhythm will be needed.

Clapping is the most obvious form of body rhythm, but ideally many parts of the body should be used. If possible, children should be given opportunities to find ways of producing sounds of their own.

For example, a group of six children was sitting on chairs in a circle putting together body sounds to make a piece. Two children had their feet flat on the floor and rocked them to produce: Toes, toes; heels, heels; toes, toes; heels, heels.

Another two children used their fingers to tap on their heads (thus hearing beautiful sounds in their heads but which were inaudible to the rest!): Fingers, fingers, fingers, fingers (two 'fingers' to each 'toes').

The last two children, who were sitting opposite to each other, made up rhythms by slapping their knees, then clapping and slapping each other's hands in the Caribbean 'high fives' greeting.

Putting rhythms with a simple song

KS1, AT1, (a), (b), (c), (d).
The simple little song below (Figure 1) is of a type known as a 'skeleton song'. It is one of those which provides the chance for children to suggest words to fit into the gaps and to use them as rhythmic accompaniments.

'What shall we have for breakfast?
What shall we have for tea?
I like _____ ,
That's the thing for me.'
If the chosen word is 'sausages', then this can be practised by all and then clapped by an accompanying group as an ostinato: Sausages, sausages, sausages, sausages. Children can then choose another food, such as 'onion bhagee', which can be used for a second verse and practised so that both rhythms can be played together by accompanying groups while the song is sung.

Any song will provide word rhythms for the purposes of accompaniment, but these should be chosen with care. For example, if singing 'Kookaburra sits on an old gum tree', it will be much better to choose 'Old gum tree, old gum tree', than 'Kookaburra sits, Kookaburra sits' if the rhythm is to be clapped. Young children tend to clap from the arm, whereas a rapid rhythm needs to be clapped from the wrist in the same way that a beater or a rhythm stick is best handled. When introducing the use of instruments, therefore, it is important to choose those which are easily manipulated and encourage accurate playing by giving an immediate response.

Introducing instruments

KS1, AT1 (b).
Suitable instruments for young children include the wood block, rhythm sticks and simple drums. Tambourines, jingles and maracas do not provide an instant response unless played skilfully so are

Figure 1

perhaps not suitable at the outset (although the first two can be useful in this context if struck but not shaken). The castanet is a glorious instrument in the hands of a skilled player but few children ever manage to use it as anything but a source of sound effects.

If, at first, children seem to find their hands 'distant' and difficult to control accurately, the extension of the appendages with the use of beaters may only compound the difficulty. This is not to say that children should be discouraged from using beaters, but the type of beater to be employed should be considered. Suppose an adult was required to play a big drum and for the purpose was given a cricket stump or a stick the size of a tenor recorder. It would seem unfair and would make the playing process an awkward business, but this is what we do when we provide a young child with a full-sized drumstick or the kind of beater commonly provided for older children.

A suitable drumstick should reach no further than the palm of the hand, if laid along the inside of the arm so that its end touches the upper arm inside the elbow. A larger stick would, in the hands of a small child, be an unwieldy burden and prevent the possibility of proper rhythmic control.

Playing from non-standard notations

KS1, AT1, PoS (i), (ii), (iv), (v), (vi), (vii), (ix) and (x).
So far, 'word rhythms' have been used as guides as to what should be played. They act as a kind of internal notation. Following from this, empty breakfast cereal packets, each containing a plastic bag of sand for stability, can be set, with the cereal name clearly visible, on a table in front of the class. These can be arranged and re-arranged to provide a kind of non-standard notation for accompanying songs or for making a rhythmic sequence.

Another form of non-standard notation can be created by using pictures of, for example, insects, as in Figure 2. After asking the children to identify the pictures and discussing the insects with them, tell them that as you point to each insect, they should speak its name twice, for example:

Caterpillar, caterpillar, butterfly, butterfly,
Grasshopper, grasshopper, bee, bee.

Make sure your hand anticipates the moment when the word is to be spoken or the class will not have time to respond.

Two rhythms at once

Divide the class into two, then use two pointers, perhaps a drumstick and a ruler, to act as signals to each group. Explain that they should speak or use body sounds only when their pointer is used.

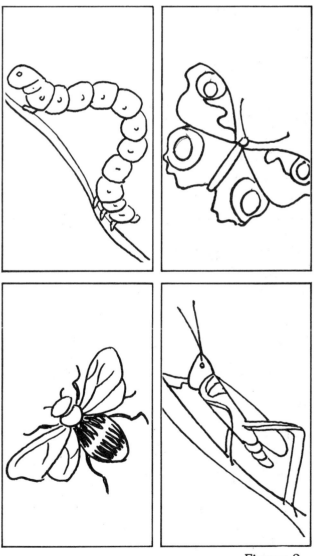

Figure 2

Use one pointer, then the other. When both pointers are used, encourage both groups to respond to the indicated rhythm at the same time so that when two different pictures are indicated, two rhythms are played concurrently. If body sounds alone are raggedly played, then it may be necessary to return to saying and playing.

Four rhythms at once

Divide the class into four and designate each quarter as caterpillars, butterflies, grasshoppers or bees. Point to the cards one at a time with a single pointer so that the group representing the picture responds. To make the responses into steady rhythms it is best to direct the children to say or clap the rhythm twice or even four times. You can then tell the children that once their picture is indicated, they are to continue to respond until told to stop, so that as each picture is indicated another group joins in. When all the children are playing, control the volume with the use of your hand and, finally, indicate whether the groups are to stop one by one, or all together.

Instruments can now be introduced into this activity. Place four types of instruments on a table at the front of the class. Decide which ones are suitable for the rhythm which they have to play. For example, the drum probably plays 'bee, bee,' most effectively while the agile rhythm sticks are better suited to playing 'caterpillar, caterpillar'. If, say, two drums, two blocks, two sets of rhythm sticks and two tambourines are chosen, place these in front of the appropriate groups. Invite two children out to play their rhythm with the rest of their group. Explain that when the class is signalled to stop, the players at the front should continue. The object is to see if they can maintain their rhythm on their own without help. Repeat the activity as necessary to ensure that all children have the chance to play instruments. The experience of playing in a small group will also enhance the ability to play instrumental accompaniments to songs.

Controlling volume levels

KS1, AT1 (b), PoS (iv) and (v).
There is a difficulty which may be encountered when children play instruments: when using body rhythms, children often refrain from playing too loudly because it tends to hurt. With

instruments, however, there is less chance of this and consequently the volume tends to increase. It is therefore wise to emphasise, and give practice in, the control of volume when introducing instruments.

Playing sensitively

KS1, AT1 (c) and (d), PoS (viii) to (xii).
So far this chapter has dealt with rhythmic ability and the results of using the activities mentioned will very likely sound fairly 'hearty'. However, the ability to make a potentially noisy instrument sound softly with no loss of rhythmic clarity needs practice and here the triangle, suspended cymbal and drum or tambourine tapped with the finger can be used to good effect. This gentle kind of playing will no doubt have been discovered in listening activities when the variety of sounds able to be produced by an instrument was explored. Furthermore, games like the Tambourine Race, mentioned in Chapter 2, will have encouraged delicate and controlled use of the hands and fingers. Stories which encourage sensitivity in playing incidental music can be devised and, as fine movements of the body are encouraged in physical education and dance, so the improvisation of music to go with the dance will involve equally controlled movements.

Composition, improvisation and the discussion which is needed to plan a piece can provide practice in the production of a range of sound qualities. It may be that a sound needs gradually to get louder, to die away, or slow down and stop. The encouragement of the necessary physical skills may be introduced in a whole class situation, but they are best explored in small groups.

This kind of work is most effective when the children are familiar with the instruments and have had a good deal of practice in handling them through listening and compositional activities.

In one school some new instruments were brought into a Y1 class. The teacher

was horrified at the children's reaction since they gleefully seized the instruments and hammered away in a manner that was, to say the least, unmusical. The headteacher, who was a music specialist, suggested that this was just a passing phase and that small groups should be allowed to experiment with the instruments during activity time when it could be suggested that to play too loudly would disturb others. This avoided a negative attitude being taken to children who were, she hoped, merely experimenting and discovering. Within three weeks the children found that there were many other attractive ways of approaching the use of the instruments and, though little formal use had yet been made of the instruments, the children had learned a great deal. Rubber beaters, which had been allowed to strike and dwell on the bars of a glockenspiel so that nothing but an ugly 'clunk' was heard, were now allowed to bounce and the pleasing sound of a clear and continuing note taught them how the beater really ought to be used.

The graphic notation of effects requiring sensitive playing will involve simple musical signs so that variations in volume (dynamics) can be recorded beside the symbols which represent the sounds. When children have experimented to see what variety of sounds can be produced from an instrument, they should be encouraged to invent symbols so that their musical intention can be communicated to other players. Figure 3 is copied from Natalie's

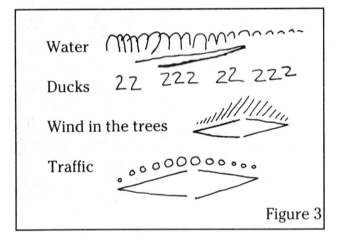

Figure 3

piece which was part of a composition based on a walk in a Birmingham park. This part of the walk began where the water of a small lake overflowed noisily into a drain and continued past a small duck-inhabited island on which grew willow trees; there was a road running by and a fair breeze blowing. The section before had ended with a crescendo in the water sound, and the signs for crescendo ⊂ and decrescendo ⊃ had just been learned.

Natalie's chosen instruments were a shaken tambourine for the water, wood blocks for the ducks, maracas for the wind and a drum for the traffic. These had to be handled very carefully as the teacher's pointer passed along the paper score. The crescendo may have been rather 'lumpy' and the passing cars may have sounded in poor health, but the exercise was clearly enjoyable and satisfying to the players, whose skill was tested to the limit.

Fair shares for all

In this kind of activity, it is important to make sure that everyone gets the chance to practise their playing skills. Too often a group of 'experts' emerges in a class and then careful watch needs to be kept to see that the less able are not branded by the more able as mere 'hewers of wood and drawers of water'.

Care is also needed to make sure that the 'butch' little boy, who can so easily feel silly and develop a 'humorously' ham-handed method of playing to hide his blushes, is encouraged to be sensitive. He needs to have his efforts appreciated and to be encouraged. It is so easy always to let Emma play the glockenspiel because she is so much better at it than anyone else. With music it is often tempting to consider the end product and to pay less regard to the process of putting the piece together.

If a child seems to be reluctant to take part in a musical activity it is likely that he has already made an assessment of his own abilities and is in the process of opting out. That is why it is important to encourage him to do well in relation to his personal yardstick and to make sure that he has that opportunity to do so.

Chapter 5
Vocal skills

'Pupils should sing a variety of simple unison songs with some control of breathing, dynamics and pitch' [AT1, KS1, PoS (iii)].

This chapter is not concerned with the improvement of children's singing, but rather with the considerations which need to be given to children who may be put off and never begin to sing at all.

'Tone deafness'

Although a beautiful voice may be a gift, this is largely a matter of voice quality and not the ability, or inability, to use what one is born with. People can be born with the equipment, but still not learn to sing in tune, which is a result of aural experience, encouragement and practice.

This tends to attract the totally inappropriate label of 'tone deafness'. Whether a person has a potentially good voice or not has nothing to do with her ability to sing in tune.

Adults who cannot sing in tune, and who frequently admit to suffering as a result, can be taught to do so. Very little assistance is needed to help them, once the mountainous task of overcoming shyness, dread – almost guilt – is achieved. The actual problem invariably dates from very early in their lives but their resistance to do something about it has been steadily built up by comments and situations throughout their lives as people around them make remarks which they think are funny. As one lady who was being helped remarked, 'If you are fat, or have spots, or one leg longer than the other, no one is supposed to say anything, but if you can't sing in tune, anyone can take the mickey – and it hurts.'

Deaf people, who have learned to speak but cannot hear themselves, speak in a monotone, as do sufferers from a rare condition called disphonia which can be truly described as tone deafness.
In fact, many who would call themselves 'tone deaf' have musical and well-modulated speaking voices. They do, however, seem to share one characteristic. This, in both men and women, is that they have voices of low pitch – the natural altos and basses of society. One must not think that this was something that developed in teenage years. One can detect differences in children's voices when they come to the reception class and it is here that first failure to sing in tune can take place and the insidious process of feeling bad about it begin. One careless remark from a teacher who thinks that all children can sing in the higher range if they put their mind to it, and the seeds of self-doubt are sown.

Parents' influence

Why is it that some children come to school able to sing while others do not? It is not a matter of genes, though non-singing parents who do not care to sing to their child can be of little help. When a mother or father sings to a child, it is most likely that a lower pitch, which is recommended as a starting point for all, will be adopted because it is usually in the intimate 'having a cuddle' situation that these singing sessions take place. The lower pitch is the tone of warmth and gentle communication and a little reflection on similar situations will confirm that this is so. Sweet nothings delivered in a squeaky voice by either

communicant are likely to have a detrimental effect upon the moment instead of the effect which is intended.

The singing parent unconsciously chooses a pitch that the child can manage and in no time little in-tune grunts reward the 'teacher' and the game turns into an invaluable lesson, repeated again and again to the considerable satisfaction of both parties. This has been observed in very young children who, despite having hardly five words in their vocabulary, achieved quite complicated feats of pitching:
Parent: (*singing*) 'One, two, three, four –'
Child: 'Five' (*wobbling on to the note*).
Parent: 'Once I caught a fish a –'
Child: 'Live' etc.

In this situation there can be no unfavourable comparison with another child and the 'singing lessons' are conducted according to the needs of the individual child in a way that could hardly be improved upon by a skilled teacher.

Developing voice range

Echo games

All young children need, at first, to practise using the lower part of their voice range (B below middle C up to F, see Figure 1).

Figure 1

This doesn't provide much room for songs, but little echo games and rhymes, such as that below, will provide the opportunity for instant success so that the goal of reaching G will not seem insuperable to those with lower-pitched voices.

Teacher : I hear an echo.
     E D   E C
Children: I hear an echo.
     E D   E C
Teacher : Who are you?
      E D E
Children: Who are you?
      E D E
Teacher : Hallo, echo.
     E D E C
Children: Hallo, echo.
     E D E C
Teacher : How do you do?
      E D   C
Children: How do you do?
      E D   C

Singing questions

Question and answer games, similar in format to the 'Say what I say' and 'Clap what I clap' activities described in the previous chapter, are most valuable at the outset and these should be pitched around middle C, D and E. (Notes can be taken from chime bars.) The following exchange provides an example of a singing question game:

Teacher: Hallo, everyone.
          C D E
Children: Hallo, Miss.
          C D E
Teacher: How are you today?
          C   D E
Children: Very well, thank you.
          C D   E
Teacher: What is the weather like?
          E   D   E   C
Children: It is raining.
          E D E C
Etc.

In one Birmingham school, the headteacher had been trained to take part; when he entered a room, the teacher would sound a middle C on the chime bar, which she also used as a stop routine, and a short, three-part choral greeting session would take place. The class response would include those children who spoke little English but who clearly took part with a will.

It has been observed that children for whom English is a second language and who are shy about displaying their

Pass the message

Messages can be passed round three or four groups, or as many as the teacher thinks suitable. The following example shows how a message can be passed on:

```
Teacher:   'I have a message, pass it on.'
           E D    E  C    E D E
Group 1:   'I have a message, pass it on.'
(echo)     E D    E  C E    D E
Group 2:   'I have a message, pass it on.'
(echo)     E D    E  C  E   D E
Teacher:   'If you're wearing something
           E     D      E
           red, please stand up.'
           C  E    D     E
```
Etc.

These activities are not very different from some of the aural tests included in instrumental grade examinations. For example, in the aural tests for Grade 2 standard, candidates are required to sing a group of three notes played twice by the examiner.

It is often the practice of some instrumental teachers to concentrate upon aural tests only shortly before an examination which, together with the small proportion of marks awarded for this skill, suggests that it is not too important. On the other hand, some teachers regularly administer such tests to see if a child is to be taken on as a pupil, thus making it look as if the ability to pitch a note is held in the highest regard.

Obviously a balanced view is needed. However, it is undoubtedly true that the attainment of this skill in the early years will lead to the successful development of a wide range of musical activities during school life.

Stretch a word

Alternative uses of the voice come largely into the field of composing, and these will be discussed in Chapter 6, but the following 'word-stretching' activity which encourages children to sustain vocal sounds and to

linguistic ability, will sing quite unselfconsciously in this kind of activity. A little boy from Sri Lanka, who arrived in the middle of term unable to speak or understand any English, sang a good deal in the new language learned by rote before he tried his first faltering words in spoken communication.

The individual's confidence needs to be built up by taking part in whole class activities. Then the class can be divided so that the responsibility for the reply falls upon increasingly smaller groups of children. Thus the moment when a solo response may be required is prepared for gently.

exercise their vocal cords without embarrassment should be considered here.

Say to the children: 'Halloooooooooooooooooooooooooooooooo', and encourage them to repeat it. Go on to ask: 'Whoooooooooooooooooooooooooooo would like their name streeeeeeeetched?'

When children offer their names, let the whole class join in with 'stretching'. The result doesn't sound much like music, but knowledge of what the voice will do, or can be made to do, increases.

Choosing suitable songs

It is clear that teachers should choose songs which are of a suitable range for children at the start of their singing lives. The list of publications in the Resources section (page 179) contains much suitable material and publishers today are clearly aware of children's needs. Problems sometimes occur when well-known traditional songs are used without consideration of this matter. One excellent reception teacher had among her enthusiasms (which included fostering sharing, politeness to others, being helpful and kind and looking at the world in wide-

eyed wonder) the desire to keep the old nursery rhymes alive. She had a beautiful soprano voice and some of her children soon began to be noticed and marked down for future membership of the choir. Her favourite nursery rhyme was 'Humpty Dumpty'. This song has a huge range (eleven notes from top to bottom), and if sung at a pitch so that middle infants had a chance of reaching the top note, the lowest note sounded at a pitch of which a grown man could be proud. Conversely, if the singing pitch was raised to make the bottom note singable by infants, cathedral choir boys would be needed to reach the top note.

It is sad that 'growlers' are allowed to continue by teachers who simply do not know that the problem is avoidable. Moreover, the child often has no idea that there is a problem until someone laughs at his efforts.

Range of notes

The choice of songs in the reception year is therefore crucial and the feature which must be most importantly considered is their range, the distance between highest to lowest notes.

'One, two, three, four, five, once I caught a fish alive', starting on E, will take the singers no higher than G, though it goes

down to A below middle C. This does not matter as much as notes going too high because no one ever seems to have been made into a 'growler' by being made to sing too low.

Stepwise songs

A further consideration in choosing a song is that care should be taken to see that there are not large 'jumps' in the tune from a low note to a high note and vice versa. Songs that use the notes of the scale in a stepwise fashion, as does 'One, two, three, four, five', are much more suitable since the adjustment of the vocal cords from one note to the next is relatively slight. 'Pop goes the weasel' can be seen to present greater problems in this respect, and 'A froggie would a-wooing go', using the old English tune, is totally unsuitable.

Cumulative songs

While wishing to use songs which would give plenty of practice in singing, teachers will recognise the difficulties which younger children may encounter when several verses are involved. Some will manage to learn them but others will be put off, so 'cumulative' songs, which add a little to the basic verse each time it is sung, are

most useful. An example of this kind of cumulative song is 'One man went to mow' and it is, as many cumulative songs are, valuable also as reinforcement to counting ability.

Skeleton songs

'Skeleton' songs are also valuable because the basic words remain the same but words chosen by the children to fill the gaps can provide an endless supply of verses. The best known of these is 'Old MacDonald had a farm'. The notes of this 'jump' about and it is, therefore, not an obvious choice for the first term. It does tend, also, to encourage the children to shout, so it should be approached with care. 'The wheels on the bus' and 'What shall we have for breakfast?', mentioned earlier, are useful and many similar songs can be found in *This Little Puffin* and publications by the National Playgroups Association.

Popular songs

It is sometimes tempting to think that children need to be presented with contemporary, modern songs and will think the songs sung by past generations of young children silly. This is clearly not true, though attempts to choose songs with

this approach may produce such an attitude in the children. Many 'pop-type' songs, not written specifically for young children, contain difficult rhythms and are not conducive to smooth singing, which needs to be mastered before other styles are attempted.

Teaching songs to children

The best way of teaching a song to any children, and certainly the most time-effective, is simply to sing the song over and over, encouraging the whole class to join in.

Teaching the song in bits, the first words, then the next phrase, then the next words, and so on generally ensures that the first part of the song is best known and by all the children. As the song goes on, however, fewer and fewer will be able to keep pace, and the least able singers will derive little benefit. On the other hand, to sing the whole song repeatedly gives the opportunity for the more timid singers to take their time, and as the sound grows, as more voices grow more confident, the stimulus to sing also grows greater. It may be that teachers begin to get the feeling that the song has been repeated too many times and think that enough is enough. One must remember, however, that it is only the best singers who have been singing for most of the repeats and that, with each repeat, more children will be able fully to take part.

Two schools in Surrey were three miles apart. The children at Pyrford sang like angels, while the children at Broadmere seemed not to have the same ability. The teacher at Broadmere observed his colleague teaching a song. She seemed to take so long repeating the song after it was apparently known. Then, realising the children's real need, he returned to his school 'a sadder and a wiser man'. That afternoon his children sang as never before.

Using commercial tapes

There are a number of companies now producing tapes which accompany song books and these are most useful. The best way of encouraging singing is to sing oneself: this can be practised with one of the tapes intended for use in class.

These tapes, especially those which offer to take over the whole task of teaching a song, will be more effective if the teacher sings along with the class. This joining in will help teachers who are concerned about their own singing ability because practice of this sort does improve singing skills irrespective of age.

Using rounds

Rounds can provide valuable singing practice and the children clearly enjoy taking part in this kind of music-making. One needs to be careful, however, that 'round readiness' is reached before attempting this kind of music. Chapter 10 discusses the use of rounds in detail and also suggests ways in which instrumental work can be incorporated.

Remedial work

Growlers

Of course one finds 'growlers' in one's class, both in the infant and the junior school, who will have missed the opportunity to begin singing. It seems that boys are more frequent sufferers than girls. In one Yorkshire school, a boy's classmates had noticed the growling sound he made during singing activities, and one of them approached the teacher, saying, 'Sir, Chris sings right low, dun't ee, Sir!'

The teacher reacted quickly with, 'I expect that when he grows up he'll have a great big deep voice. Perhaps if he sits with you and David, you can help him to sing the high notes.'

The potential giant and his new-found friends, who had been about to become his critics, made sure that they joined forces whenever singing took place and, in that case, the strategy worked.

Helping individuals

One particular method of helping children and adults alike has been used for several years and has often proved successful. This requires a one-to-one situation. The person being helped is encouraged to sing any note. This is played on the piano by the helper and the singer is asked to repeat the sound, which is again played. Because the note sung was of the singer's choice, there is no embarrassment in being wrong. The piano note follows the voice, enabling the singer to listen to the note she has just sung. The practice of playing a note and asking the singer to produce it can often compound the problem by increasing her sense of failure. It is at these moments that one invariably discovers that the singer has a preference for a lower pitch than would be chosen by someone who can sing in tune. It is often that one finds that the so-called 'tone deaf' have control of their pitching, but only of a few low notes which are not likely to be part of a classroom song. When the notes with which the singer is happy are established, she can be asked to echo three-note phrases within that pitch range. Gradually, higher notes can be added and, in a ten-minute session, the controllable range will be widened upwards by three notes. This process must not be hurried and a session must be arranged every day. The positive reinforcement of any advance is the key to success and a great many 'hopeless' cases have thus become useful members of the choir.

St George's telephone

A certain device, which is an example of the kind of equipment which can usefully link music and science, has been most successful both in class and in a choir.

This is 'St George's Telephone', named after the Redditch church where it was first used. The 'telephone' is essentially a cardboard receiver which carries the voice from mouth to ear. It can be made from cardboard tubes such as those in the centre of rolls of cooking foil (Figure 2). Its use is combined with the activity described above and it has had considerable and sometimes instant success.

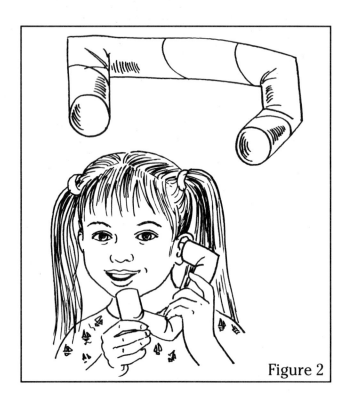

Figure 2

All the children should be given the opportunity to use the 'telephone' to hear their voices as they sing, but the 'growlers' seem to derive the greatest benefit from the use of this instrument. The opportunity to hear what the voice is doing and to 'feel' what the vocal cords are doing at the same time seems to be what is required.

Encouraging singing

There is one final point about encouraging singing. In all school activities, it is desirable to encourage best efforts and the most satisfactory outcome. Demand clear words and loud and soft response as appropriate. Let the children hear themselves on tape and encourage them to assess their own performances. They will judge the outcome for themselves and the process will be educationally valuable.

Chapter 6
The beginnings of composition

'The development of the ability to perform and compose music with understanding.' (AT1)

Before the 1950s

Those sufficiently elderly to remember what it was like to be at school before 1944 will no doubt recall, in the early years in an elementary school, how seldom one was required to write 'a composition'. The author recalls every word of his single offering from that time, which was on the subject of 'My Pet', based on the only 'pet' he had – a glove puppet monkey.

To write one's own work in those days was far rarer than copying from the board or learning a short poem or hymn, which afterwards had to be written from memory. Music was almost exclusively singing from

Songs for the Forces, which was greatly enjoyed, but there was also a little singing from tonic sol-fa notation and occasionally a wind-up gramophone squeaked distantly from Mrs Harding's desk.

To have suggested that children might make up their own music at that time would have produced the response that it might be possible if they were first to learn the piano.

A new approach

By the 1950s, a wind of change was blowing through language work and in the 1960s Chatto & Windus produced a book called *The Excitement of Writing*, which was a collection of children's creative writing.

It has been said that this time of 'freedom' was responsible for a decline in some of the language skills which figure prominently in today's National Curriculum. This was no doubt the case, but at the same time that spelling was accorded a far less prominent position than now, so the dreaded rules of musical composition were seen for what they were: iron templates which were designed to produce more eighteenth-century-style music.

In the 1950s, a child who composed a tune stood a good chance of being 'wrong' and received the advice that real composers had to study hard before being able to get it right. It was even suggested by an otherwise excellent music teacher that Benjamin Britten was only a flash in the pan because he hadn't graduated via the route which led through the cathedral organ loft.

That wind of change which began to blow so long ago has now reached every subject area, and even resulted in the addition of an exciting new curriculum area, technology. Reception children's thoughts are recorded in a variety of ways, efforts are made to use mathematics creatively and children research and draw conclusions in the areas of humanities and environmental studies. The creative arts have shaken off the ball-and-chain of technique as a first priority, and children now begin to compose music in their first days at school.

Developing a music vocabulary

Musical composition is a kind of communication, but it does not necessarily transmit a message to the listener as a descriptive piece of writing may. It does, however, say, 'This is how I feel about', and in this music is fortunate because, as in dance, children can easily understand the expressive quality which is an important element of the work.

At the same time, it is necessary for these thoughts and feelings to be translated into music via language and so discussion of sounds made from all kinds of sources – table-tops, saucepans and plastic containers – must take place with consideration of differing sound qualities and the words which describe them. In teacher-led listening activities, children can be invited to make long sounds and shorter sounds and to think about likely connections between sounds and movements and textures. Some of these connections come easily, though conventions such as high and low sounds may initially prove confusing ('The mouse story', on page 171, was specifically invented to teach this concept).

It is important to provide early playing experience using classroom instruments to introduce children to the idea of playing

loud and soft sounds and to encourage them to play sounds reflecting different moods.

Sound qualities, expressed in the children's own words and played on chosen instruments, all lead to a knowledge of the resources available to the would-be composer and, if asked the right questions, the children will make thoughtful and personal responses.

Simple sound pictures

'By the end of key stage 1, pupils should be able to investigate, choose and combine sounds to produce simple compositions.'

'I am going to show Sarah a picture of an animal. She will choose an instrument and try to tell you about the animal by playing.'

Sarah plays.

'Is it a big animal or a small animal? Is it a quick animal or slow? Is it fierce or cuddly? Now, you can tell us, Sarah, why you made it sound like that.'

Unlike the young writer of a tune years ago, Sarah cannot be wrong. Her reasons may not tie up with anyone else's opinion, but those who both agree or disagree will be stimulated to think about how and what they will play when their turn comes.

It will be a matter of time before the young child's BANG BANG BANG BANG *fortissimo* on the biggest drum available to represent an elephant walking, softens into a perception of the infinite grace and poise with which the animal conducts itself. This is not important, since what the child is really saying is 'BIG BIG BIG BIG' and that is valuable. Also, even if the young child has seen a live elephant, he has probably not really 'looked' at one: to see is not to look.

At story-time, Richard made the music for the giant coming into the forest.

'Is the giant walking quickly or slowly? What can Richard do to make the giant seem to come nearer and nearer?'

Richard got up and took the drum to the far end of the classroom and then approached, playing as he came. The

teacher grinned because his idea was better than hers!

'Can you make it sound like that without getting up?'

Richard, however, had decided that that was how it needed to be. The idea of crescendo was not yet linked in his mind with approaching footsteps.

One of the outcomes of this work was that some Y5 children, after seeing the infant assembly that resulted from this activity, decided that *they* would make a composition which involved moving from place to place while playing. They produced a haunting composition of great beauty, worked on at lunchtimes and without interference by a teacher.

Discussing by playing

Thinking about a topic through the composition of related music is valuable because it allows children to examine and re-examine an idea from different perspectives and with different senses. Writing about an idea is not as good as writing *and* making part of a frieze. Add to this drama, dance, modelling and music, and the children, who do not all respond to the same kind of stimulus, will be likely to know, to understand, to talk about and to make predictions about the basic idea because of one or two curriculum experiences which enhanced the others.

It is important that music should not be regarded as habitually assisting 'more important' subjects. There is a danger of reverting to the dominance of the core subjects with servant subjects nailed on here and there. The process of encouraging children to think is, in itself, valuable in helping them to deal with the whole curriculum. If science and mathematics can provide an impetus to a child's musical composition, the outcome is of equal value to the musical device which underpins the understanding of multiplication.

Using environmental sounds

It is possible to assess a child's progress by noting her response to environmental sounds. In making the child aware of these sounds, both great and small, and encouraging her to discriminate and discuss, you foster in her a valuable ability.

A colleague spoke of walking by a busy city junction and detecting the voice of a kestrel high in the sky. Once you have encouraged children to listen for the lesser sounds among the greater, what better response could be made than the making of a composition which describes the sound picture?

A tape recorder can be used or the children can be asked to recall, over a period of about half a minute, what was heard and in what order the sounds came. Discussion of the sound scenario should follow, after which the choice of instruments, body or vocal sounds can be made.

'Were there sounds which happened only sometimes? Was there anything that you could hear all the time? What was the loudest? The softest? The shortest? Did anything grow louder? What happened then? Can anyone think of anything else? How can we make sure our piece lasts the same time?'

A long graphic score can be put on the wall and used to play from, with the teacher or a child 'conducting' with a pointer.

It may be that after a walk round a small park or even the playground, a map showing the main features can be drawn and the sounds heard at various places recalled. This ties up very nicely with mapping and journeys, and though very small children's maps pay little regard to scale, judicious use of the pointer can maintain a continuous performance. Alternatively, the teacher can produce a basic map on to which the sources of remembered sounds can be drawn.

Mapping a story made up by the children

will introduce the idea of sequencing events. I can remember a journey underground to the lair of a sleeping dragon producing beautifully eerie effects and tense faces as the players re-lived the terrors of the darkness.

The performance of such a piece and its recording and use in movement provides something akin to firsthand experience. Subsequent writing and picture-making tends to be all the more vivid. Mole in the Wild Wood, Toad on the train, passages from *The Hobbit*, Shelob's Lair from *The Lord of the Rings* and similar material have, at various levels of the primary age range, been explored and enjoyed.

Composition and mood

**'Pupils should create, select and organise sounds in response to different stimuli'
[KS1, AT1, PoS (ix)].**

Before children can reasonably be asked to make up a piece describing mood, it is good to consider their reaction to pieces of recorded music and to establish that such a thing is possible.

'How does it make you feel?' is a useless question to ask a child who has never considered that music might evoke specific emotions. Interesting and relevant questions have to be framed so that the child has a genuine reason for listening and subsequently putting her feelings into her own music. 'If you had composed this music, how might you have been feeling when you wrote it?' is a possible question for an experienced junior to consider, but relating the right question to the child's experience is a delicate matter.

The concept of moods being expressed in music has often been introduced by suggesting that the music was heard on television, and that the children must listen carefully and try to guess what the programme was about. In so abstract a medium as music, the concept of mood can tend sometimes to produce unconsidered responses which the children think will please the teacher. However, once they have considered the basic possibilities – happy, sad, frightening, dreamy – and proved that they really are thinking, outlandish suggestions must be tested by democratic discussion. If 'Morning' from Grieg's *Peer Gynt* Suite is thought to be appropriate music for a film about a witch, and it can be argued that there are good reasons for the decision, then that's what it will have to be. Grieg's original intention for the piece had nothing to do with fiords, clear mountain air or Norway, so ascribing meaning to music is clearly purely subjective.

Composition using work cards

Work cards for group compositions are useful and may be used when reading skills and other musical considerations make them appropriate. Written instructions might seem more appropriate to the junior age range, but in real group work, where all contribute and learn from each other, the use of an appropriate work card in addition to verbal instructions will provide useful language practice.

A further consideration would be whether the children are used to responsibility-sharing group work. If they are not, composition is probably not the best activity by which it may be introduced. Though juniors will clearly need less verbal explanation than infants when working from work cards, it is good to introduce young children to this method of working. The level of work is a matter which must be left to the discretion of the individual teacher and the unique needs of her class. The following suggestions can be used on work cards for groups of children.

● Make a happy piece for a drum, a tambourine and a wood block.
● Make a piece which starts with a tambourine playing softly. A drum joins in and then a wood block. Make them all do different things and end together.
● Take chime bars C, D and E, a drum, a tambourine and wood block. Make up a piece about your favourite foods using word rhythms. Make sure that the rhythms fit together and that the tune can be heard.

If these are introduced as whole class activities, the instruments should be on a table at the front of the class and the players should come to them. Once the players have come out to the front, sections of the class can help them by clapping. The rhythms can be practised initially by the divided class before players come out to be soloists.

Once these activities have been practised in the whole class situation with volunteers taking turns in trying out pieces so that all are aware of what is required, a different requirement can be given to each group.

Management of group work

Instructions need to be clear, precise and of a kind which require a response which can be checked by the teacher. 'Think about foods about which you can make music,' will stimulate little effort; the following procedure is far more likely to meet with success.

Say to the children, 'I want you to take three minutes to decide which foods (or whatever) you are going to choose and to try the sounds of their names speaking them.' (Instruments should be out of reach at this point.) It is always a good idea to impose a time limit. That and a clear instruction keep the work flowing; by controlling the amount of time available, one can assess how successful the attempt at building up group skills is. During this discussion circulate among the children to demonstrate an interested presence and to keep an eye on the least reliable groups. At the end of the specified time, say, 'Right! Now let's hear what the first group is using.' Let the first group reply, then say, 'Let's hear you put them together.' Assist them in their performance if necessary and then turn to the following groups, inviting assessment by the other children and offering them encouragement.

When all the groups have had the chance to describe their work, say, 'Now you can pick up the instruments and put your piece together. Five minutes to get it right.' The time allowed should, of course, be as long as you feel is necessary. If the activity is running smoothly, allow it to continue, but if not, it may be necessary to gather the class together to review progress.

At the end of the working time, allow each group to perform its piece. Explain to the class that politeness must be extended to the performers, while they should be encouraged to announce the name of the

piece and to play it as well as possible. The announcement is particularly important if a recording is being made because, as the tape fills up, it will be difficult to remember who did what. For this reason, it is also useful to give the reading of the counter on the tape machine so that any piece can be referred to without delay.

At another time, perhaps at the next music lesson, play the taped compositions and discuss how they could be improved. This re-working can be done at odd moments when all the players are free and the result re-recorded if desired.

Accommodation for group work

It is often affirmed that children can work at group composition in the same room. This may be true, although it is by no means desirable. One alternative is to make use of separate spaces near the classroom,

but this will make supervision difficult unless the children can really be trusted. Another is to try to book the hall, which may be big enough to allow for separation between groups. Failing this, one must rely upon the children's ability to discriminate between the sounds that concern them and those that don't; if this cannot be achieved, the exercise will be less valuable.

Music for a video presentation

KS1, AT1 (c), PoS (viii), (ix) and (x).
For Y2 children and upwards, try letting them make incidental music after watching a section of video film with the sound turned down. It may be necessary to chart the action on the screen on a time-related sheet, which is an excellent mathematical exercise. Ask the children to record moods and changes of mood then try to compose music to fit the scenario exactly. Explain that the music has to be run at exactly the right moment.

Maths, music, design technology, language and information technology come into this activity. An obvious extension would be for the children to make the video film themselves. Not only must the team work together without problems, but also must be sufficiently trustworthy to handle the equipment.

Conclusion

The greatest emphasis so far has been placed upon 'free' composition. The result of this will sound very much related to the music of the twentieth century. This is as it should be but, like adults, children do not easily disregard those melodies and harmonies which, after all, come from their cultural background.

Much of the work in this chapter, although suitable for Key Stage One, has relevance to Key Stage Two. In the same way, Chapter 15 discusses junior work, although many of the activities could be used in the infant school. Chapter 15 deals with a number of methods, different from those in this chapter, by which children can compose, and further suggestions appear in the resource section. No one method is any more valid than another, but all provide important opportunities to think and to communicate.

Chapter 7
Key stage two

How good it would be if all children arriving at the beginning of their junior school years were able to demonstrate that they could perform, compose, listen and appraise to the standards set in Key Stage One. How particularly good if this were possible in all the core and foundation subjects! But this will not be so, even to the extent that the overlapping levels allow. Teachers of year three children will therefore do well to consider the Key Stage One curriculum and to carry on work which, with the best will in the world, Key Stage One teachers have been unable to complete with all children.

On the face of it the differences between end of key stage statements of Key Stages One and Two do not convey in detail the amount of work which will be necessary during the four years of the junior age range; this can only become clear when the content and methodology is considered.

Attainment target 1: Performing and composing

End of key stage statement 1

Pupils should be able to '**Perform from notations interpreting signs, symbols and simple musical instructions.**'

The matter of notations from which children will perform may seem to suggest standard staff notation, but again (as was discussed in Chapter 1), this kind of notation is likely to be used extensively in only a minority of schools and less often still in year three. Approaches to the use of staff notation are included in Chapter 20 ('Keywords', page 158) and can work very well, but the question 'How relevant and necessary to the average child is this knowledge?' needs to be asked.

It can become relevant when a situation is set up in which the child discovers the need for such information, and indeed this often happens, but the use of rhythmic symbols in the forms of word rhythms, graphic notation, note grids and so on can cover a wide range of need, and the desire to teach staff notation to all in a formal way and without a good reason should be resisted.

It is possible that the method of using guitar chords which is dealt with at length in Chapter 15 may have been introduced at Key Stage One, but this kind of notation – note names on grids – has been much used in junior and middle schools with considerable success. The fact that, in this system, chords are played relates well to the mention of this extremely common Western cultural musical device in the Key Stage Two programme of study for attainment target 2. Furthermore, the use of electronic keyboards which are able to produce 'one-finger' chords is a further means of reinforcing the idea of chordal accompaniment and composition. One-finger chords are those produced by most electronic keyboards – for example, if the C key is pressed, the chord of C which is made up of three notes (C, E and G) will be produced.

In Chapter 20 (page 167) a further method of notation using rhythm grids is described which can be employed by the teacher to provide playing instructions or by children to record aspects of their own compositions. Simple musical instructions can be added to all these methods of musical notation. Signs that indicate 'getting louder' (_____), 'getting softer' (＿＿＿＿), pausing (𝄐), or playing quietly (*p*), strongly (*f*) or very strongly (*ff*) can be included as required and children delight in adding these to their compositions.

'Sir,' said a boy, 'How can you say "make it very sad"?' Sir said, 'Piangevolmente' (weepingly) and a week-long fashion for writing sad music had begun.

End of key stage statements 2 and 3

Pupils should be able to '**Sing and play a range of music, controlling pitch, rhythm and dynamics**' and '**Perform in a group, maintaining a simple part independently of another group.**'

Songs of greater complexity will become possible as children progress towards and through Key Stage Two. As their ability to use printed words becomes greater and a number of verses that don't have to be learned by memory can be sung, the scope for class singing widens considerably. Not, however, that children should not be encouraged to memorise songs. When a song is known by heart, the eyes of the class can be constantly on the teacher who can then have greater control over the way the song is sung. Breathing can be organised and the use of the whole dynamic range, from very soft to very strong, employed. This variation in volume should be carefully practised and the use of rounds (see Chapter 10) offers excellent opportunities in this respect. Chapter 10 also describes ways in which instruments can be incorporated into round singing which provides valuable practice in maintaining a simple part independently of another group.

Books are suggested in the published Resources section (page 179) which provide a wide range of material for playing and singing, often including also cross-curricular connections. These are described in terms which accommodate teachers of greater or lesser musical experience.

End of key stage statement 4

Pupils should be able to '**Devise and develop musical ideas within simple structures.**'

Chapter 11 contains a variety of styles in which compositions can be written. The use of the pentatonic scale is described

and an approach to the use of the chords which are the basis of Western harmony is set out in detail. This may sound like the province of a trained musician but, in fact, this approach has been used by generalist teachers with great success.

Another compositional structure discussed is the use of polyrhythms which employs its own kind of simple notation. Uses of this system range from the most basic to the infinitely varied in which all sorts of instruments and voices can be included. Simple forms and musical shapes are discussed which are related to the kind of musical organisation and form which will be met with in listening to recorded music.

End of key stage statement 5

Pupils should be able to '**Communicate musical ideas to others and record compositions through the use of notations.**'

It is hoped that, by the end of Key Stage One, children will have become used to using a cassette tape recorder and this facility should be freely available to children at Key Stage Two who are engaged in composition. The actual methods of recording on paper will have become more

sophisticated and relate to the notations with which children have become familiar. One cannot impose a method of recording if it has not become relevant to the children's experience, so it is strongly suggested that a choice of notations should grow out of composition rather than a single method of notation being imposed when it becomes necessary. Staff notation is, after all, only the system which developed from the trial and error of composers who knew how the music ought to sound and who sought a method of writing it down. To think that staff notation has reached its final form may be misguided. Like aural and written language, it is an organic being, constantly growing and changing. It already falls short of the needs of modern music and who can say what will be the requirements of the composers of world acclaim who are now about to enter the reception year.

Attainment target 2: Listening and appraising

End of key stage statement 1

Pupils should be able to '**Listen attentively to music of various kinds, recognising the**

main musical elements; distinguishing musical instruments and responding to changes in character and mood.'

As was emphasised in Chapter 1, music should not be listened to, in the first instance, in order that the sound of instruments and the style of composition should be learned. That music sounds liquid and fresh, or however it may be described, may be explained by pointing out that its quality is obtained by the use of the flute. There may be flute players in the school who are able to demonstrate this quality but the quality needs to be recognised first and the instrument investigated as a second consideration. Another sound is described as fierce and bright, or angry and hot. This is the brass section; can they make different sounds and is a trumpet recognisable in a more gentle mood? Having discussed one kind of sound in a piece which is familiar, it is possible to compare the same instruments in music in a different vein.

End of key stage statement 2

Pupils should be able to **'understand the principal features of the history of music and appreciate a variety of musical traditions.'**

The identification of instruments ought to take place as a game played by children with wider reasons for being interested than that of mere identification. As the ability to recognise an individual bird's song is sterile without knowledge of the bird's appearance and habits, so the nature of an instrument's sound and the uses to which a composer can put it should be compared and contrasted.

Chapter 17 discusses some ethnic musics and it is hoped that this will provide some assistance for teachers who are not familiar with music other than that of the Western tradition.

Chapter 8 discusses approaches to listening to music, ways of making it

relevant to children and the problems of understanding historical time spans. Again it is emphasised that the music, whether pop, ethnic, folk or classical, should be made familiar by some means before being discussed. Historical or geographical connections will hold little interest for children who have not already established some starting point of interest. Children who have taken part in *Pilgrimage*, a musical play set in mediaeval times and details of which are listed in the Resources section on page 179, will soon warm to original music of that age.

End of key stage statement 3

Pupils should be able to **'Describe, discuss and undertake simple analysis and evaluation of musical compositions and performances.'**

This area relies upon a vocabulary having been built up which can be used to discuss the nature of a piece of music. This vocabulary should have been building up from the early days of Key Stage One. Now simple statements of loud and soft, quick and slow, although important, are not enough. Questions of repetition of material and change of mood should be noted and these, having been experienced in recorded music, will be used by children and observed in others' compositions produced in the classroom.

It should be possible at this stage to discuss how a composer achieves the effect for which he aims. Chapter 8 considers the matters related to listening to music and includes examples of music which can be considered in this light. Merely telling children a composer's intention is not enough. They should attempt to face the same kind of challenges in their own composition and in doing so they will discover things about communicating with an audience and the importance of proper presentation of a performance that they cannot properly understand second-hand.

Chapter 8
Listening to music

Many people's enjoyment of, and involvement in, music seems to be purely a passive occupation without much evidence of analysis or appraisal. Many adult education evening institutes have a 'music appreciation' class which is useful encouragement to the popularisation of all kinds of music. Enrolling in such a class is an act of active participation which no doubt widens the musical view of the student, and, so long as the tutor is prepared to do more than put records on, and additionally to try to communicate her own enthusiasms, there can be no doubt that much can be gained from these sessions.

It must not be thought that these are purely 'classically' orientated, as musical areas as diverse as jazz, folk, pop and the music of Africa are, from time to time, advertised in these classes. Many ruses have been tried to make listening an activity in which there is real and personal involvement. One tutor discovered that no one had ever heard Beethoven's *Choral Symphony*, and a plot was laid to provide an experience which could never have been had in a concert hall. The first movements were examined, but when, later in the symphony, the voices were about to enter, the tutor just let the recording run. The effect upon the class of the male voice which seemed suddenly to interrupt the expected sounds, and the mighty 'Ode to Joy' sung by a huge choir produced shock, delight and even a few tears. Hardly a passive response, and one which owed its success to the way in

is a need, however, for all kinds of music to be experienced by children, so that they can make their own choices, without pressure and bigotry. This bigotry includes pressure from peer group when a certain pop group must be worshipped in order to admit the individual to the inner circle. The teacher has to find a more reasoned excuse for encouraging children to listen to music.

Relevant reasons for listening

One often remembers the occasion when a piece of music which is liked (or disliked) was first heard. There is quite likely to be some association with place, person or happening which fixes the piece in the mind of the listener and which afterwards stimulates the desire to hear the piece again. As time goes by, the enjoyment of the music for its own sake takes over but the association with that first hearing is easily recalled.

It may also be that another piece is listened to because it is by the same composer or musician responsible for a piece that is already enjoyed. Whatever the reason for listening, there is most likely a 'hook' which stimulates the attention of the listener.

That Haydn was expelled from the choir of Vienna Cathedral for bad behaviour or that Mendelssohn liked Birmingham and used to visit the city every year to stay with friends and to play the organ, is a poor excuse for listening to their music. The information will not catch the imagination of a class simply because it is not relevant to their experience.

It is therefore better, if possible, to choose music because it is relevant in some way or because it has been experienced in a situation in which it has received unselfconscious approval. Music used for a television advertisement or as the signature tune of a popular programme can help to lead the listener to a wider experience and real enjoyment. It might seem unlikely that even eleven mud-

which the music was presented. By contrast, the instruction to children to 'Listen to "good" music because it will do you good' has often been heard in school – of course, in such a case, they usually don't and it doesn't!

A varied menu of listening

'Pupils should listen to a range of instrumental and vocal music from early classical and later periods' [KS2, AT2, PoS (iii)].

Whereas adults have gained, along the way, experiences which enable them to say, 'I know what I like', though sometimes adding, 'although I don't understand music', the approach to children's music listening activities has to be very different. There need be no distinction between classical, pop, folk and traditional music as far as a listening child is concerned. There covered, lusty junior school-age lads chose, while in the showers of a sports club, to celebrate a notable victory by singing a famous Italian operatic aria. But the World Cup was recently over and Pavarotti had made the music known and relevant to millions who would otherwise have disregarded it as class-ridden, classical nonsense.

Difficulties with historical contexts

'Pupils should listen to the work of influential composers and learn something of their historical context and importance to the development of musical traditions' [KS2, AT2, PoS (iv)].

While popular music from many cultures seems to have a wide appeal and can be linked neatly with the study of people from other lands, classical music presents a difficulty which has to be addressed. In terms of the National Curriculum, the historical dimension is required to be understood. Children at both Key Stages One and Two have difficulty with the concept of the passage of historical time and very little knowledge of historical happenings since the sixteenth century. This is exemplified by an anecdote told by a student teacher, whose class was involved in a project about the Forties. She asked her tutor to be interviewed by the children about his experiences in the London blitz during the last world war. All was going well until one child asked, 'Was that when the Romans were?'

Although it would be unthinkable at primary level to approach the understanding of music of different ages in a chronological way similar to the way the history curriculum might be taught, this aspect of the music curriculum could well be linked to history. For example, a project on Tudors and Stuarts could be extended into a school production in which more children than those involved in the project could take part. A good reason for listening to the music of Matthew Locke (who secured the post of 'Master of the Kynge's Music' by directing a band by the side of the route of King Charles II's restoration procession) would be established and children might be invited to choose a piece of music by that composer to be played as the scene was recreated. While the question, 'Is this music suitable for a triumphal procession in which you will be taking part?' would provide a reason for listening, the experience of music typical of the time and participation in costume drama would help in focusing on the historical perspective. This could be emphasised by the use of a permanent time-line on the classroom wall showing the relationship of historical events – for instance, from the Romans to the birth of grandparents and up to the present day. This would enable the children to develop some understanding of the place of Mr Locke in history.

Listening spans

If your children have not practised the art of listening to music, the first attempt should not include the playing of a recording longer than 20 to 30 seconds. If the performance is live, then the children's patience will be extended by the interest of having something to see, but this does not mean that their listening concentration will have lasted to the end of the piece. Nor does it mean that the children will have known what they were listening to. But if some activity can be introduced to the process of listening, which gives a reason for children's ears to 'home in' on what is happening, the overall success of the activity will be greatly enhanced. If it is a matter of mood which the teacher uses to attract the children's attention, then this needs to be followed by an opportunity to reproduce a similar effect in their own composition. The act of sharing the problem which the composer was attempting to solve makes both the processes of listening and composition come alive.

Discussing music

'Pupils should talk about music heard in class, including their own compositions and performances' [KS2, AT2, PoS (v)].

In order for children to develop the ability to discuss in detail what is heard, opportunities for discussion will need to be engineered. Music which makes children leap up and 'discuss' its nature in dance is encouraging involvement and this has validity, but this kind of response alone is not enough. Children will need to listen carefully to a musical piece, so that later they have some success at understanding and discussing the style in composition. Providing them with reasons for listening will not only ensure that the listening activity has meaning but it will also help to increase children's possible listening span.

Discussion of mood

Play short extracts from 'Storm' from *Peter Grimes* by Benjamin Britten, the storm sequence from Beethoven's *Pastoral Symphony* and the storm in *The Flying Dutchman* by Wagner. Ask the children what the mood was and what they think was happening. Compare one piece with another. Does the sun come out after the Beethoven storm? Does it come out in the Britten? (There may be no right answers!)

Composers do not always consider the needs of first time or inexperienced listeners, as far as manageable listening duration is concerned, so careful editing on to an easily managed tape will greatly enhance the presentation of a specifically chosen passage. Recording a particular passage on tape two or three times will save that time-consuming rewind which, if the counter has not been set, invariably arrives at the wrong place. This multi-recording technique is important because the reason for listening needs to be changed, or reinforced, for the second and subsequent hearings and any break in continuity is unfortunate. The first focus may be, 'What might be on the television

screen if this music was played with the picture?' The second focus might be, 'Does the composer use high or low notes to give the impression of a high wind?'

Children with some knowledge and experience might be able to say that, in the Britten piece, the strings were used to depict the wind screaming in the rigging of ships at anchor, while in the Beethoven, the timpani produce the effect of a massive clap of thunder. In the Wagner, since the whole scene is observed from a wooden merchantman, it might be noticed that much of the rhythmic writing depicts the motion of the ship which plunges and rears as the savage wind tears the sails to shreds.

If the strings were used to depict screaming wind in the Britten, have they the same effect in *On Hearing the First Cuckoo in Spring* by Frederick Delius? The actual sound of the cuckoo comes a long way into the piece, so consideration of the mood of the first part, which has often been said to epitomise the peace of the English countryside (Delius wrote it in France!) can be made before that later passage when the cuckoo is heard. Tell the children to 'Listen carefully to see if you can hear a wind instrument. Does anyone know what the clarinet was pretending to be?' Let the children listen to the cuckoo in the *Pastoral Symphony* and encourage them to compare the pieces.

Having discussed the composer's intentions in a particular piece of music which was played to the children, it is possible to allow them to tell their own story in music. The questions which had been asked by the teacher to identify a focus for listening to the composer's piece now become cues in the children's own composition process.

Programme music

There are many pieces of classical music, written in the nineteenth century, which contain what musicologists call a 'programme'. Programme music follows some kind of story. For example, the story of 'Till Eulenspiegel's Merry Pranks', which is best known through the orchestral piece by Richard Strauss, is based on the traditional tale of a Flemish practical joker. After a number of escapades, Till is caught and, despite pleadings that all he did was in fun, he is hanged.

Another piece with a strong programme is *Vltava* by Smetana. This orchestral piece describes the birth of the river Vltava as a tiny stream which grows and grows until, as a broad and majestic river, it flows through Prague and on to the sea.

Perhaps the most widely known example of music with a programme is *Peter and the Wolf* by Prokofiev. This is often performed with a narration which tells the story of how a little Russian boy captures a wolf. Each character in the story is represented by specific themes played on particular instruments – the bassoon for Peter's grandfather, strings for Peter, a flute for a bird and the French horn for the wolf.

This kind of music provides a listening focus that children can understand, though care should be taken to see that children realise that not all music has some sort of narrative meaning. Programme music, nevertheless, offers them a means to consider what is heard, and stimulates thoughts and words by which it can be discussed. It also helps the child to envisage a means by which his own compositions can achieve a unity and purpose.

Music without a programme

Music without a programme can equally well be discussed, though in terms of mood and effect. The second movement of Elgar's 'cello concerto was used in a movement lesson and, though possessing no programme, the children were able to discuss its light and shade in movement and language and later in art.

When a piece by one of the 'minimalist' composers, such as Steve Reich or Philip Glass, is played the response of the individual has to be both imaginative and

abstract. Any teacher who wishes to use this kind of music should take the opportunity to experience the music herself, as the children will hear it. To do this, a proper listening situation should be set up so that the music can be listened to without fear of interruption, thus sharing the experience and gaining an insight into what the children may say upon hearing the piece. Headphones are an excellent way of achieving this, although the effect upon the listener can be somewhat soporific, not to say hypnotic, and this music is best heard sitting down at home. Your feelings will not necessarily be the same as the children's, but you need to listen to these magical textures with as much care as you will require of the children.

Minimalism may be thought of as an experimental type of music. It involves the constant simultaneous playing of a number of short equal phrases of melody which together rely upon the ear for their effect of

constant repetition. As the piece progresses, subtle changes or additions are made but, in the trance-like state which this kind of music produces upon the listener, one begins to hear 'aural illusions' which may vary from one member of the audience to another. A listening period of at least one minute is desirable, since some time is needed to receive the initial impression before the music begins to play tricks on the ear, so the children would need to be more experienced listeners who can keep their concentration at a good level. 'What do you see in your mind's eye? What did you hear? What changes did you notice?' will all produce useful responses. Encourage the children to indicate silently when they hear changes in the sound taking place. These will be mostly those which the composer has written in, but sometimes it will be noticed that a number of children share the impression of change in sound where there is none.

These approaches work well in relation to music of the nineteenth and twentieth centuries, but it is desirable for a range of music to be experienced which includes the less 'helpful' centuries. Earlier music did not set out to be descriptive. Beethoven's *Moonlight Sonata* was not so called by him, but by his publishing editor, who must have thought the title would help it sell. Attempts have been made to make music attractive to children by this means, but to hang apocryphal stories on compositions by Hadyn and Mozart, and to try to attract children's attention to their music by relating anecdotes about the composers' childhoods, is likely to be irrelevant to children who live in a different age and culture.

Situations can be set up in which the music is allowed to speak for itself. 'Going into assembly music' can be of considerable value in this respect, providing a disciplined listening atmosphere is established. This means that children entering the hall would, by school tradition, understand that music which was being played at an unobtrusive volume was there to be listened to; not to be talked

over but, by its presence, signalling that this was a quiet time when, until turned down so that the assembly could begin, listening was paramount. Familiarity with a piece of music which, in a direct 'listen to this' situation would be disregarded, often arouses interest.

One junior school used to treat this moment in the school day as a specific listening time and this was so successful that the music teacher decided to extend the activity. The five days of the week were used in order to play music of the sixteenth, seventeenth, eighteenth, nineteenth and twentieth centuries and the board on the stage would read, for example, 'Today's music is by Mozart – he lived about 200 years ago.' After a time, the teacher began to enquire which kind of music the children liked best. The nineteenth century seemed most popular, though the sixteenth century ran a close second, possibly because of the support of recorder players, some of whom had played original sixteenth century music. *Ionization* by Varese, which contains, among other things, factory sounds,

produced an interested, if slightly smirking, attention. During its first playing, a trumpet player leaned over to the teacher behind the piano and hissed, 'Is that music, Sir?' 'Sir' nodded, but a lively discussion followed at break, and some pretty abrasive comments were tried out in the following days.

The value of authentic recordings

When sharing the music of other cultures, children will sing and play enthusiastically, but unless their related listening is carefully directed to good quality equipment, they may not notice the difference between their own performance and that of the authentic group. If good listening experiences can be provided, a feeling for the musical tradition can be established and an understanding of the people's way of life built up. A good activity is to learn a song of which you also have a recording by a genuine folk or ethnic group. The song should be learned before the recording is heard so that the children are later able to recognise the difference between their performance and the real ethnic style. Discussion of how future classroom performances can be made more stylistically correct will need to take place, and there will need to be careful listening research to find how the accompaniment is to be played. It may be possible that small touches in the recorded performance, peculiar to the tradition or composer, are quite impossible to record on paper and that these can be passed on only by aural tradition, and only careful listening will reveal this. A fairly recent musical sound which is still very popular illustrates this. The real flavour of the music played by the Glenn Miller Orchestra was produced partly by characteristic relationships between the instruments, but these can be reproduced without capturing the essential quality of the band. The greatest element in the style was the orchestra's ability to make variations in rhythm and note length which could not be recorded on paper, but only passed on in an aural tradition from conductor to band, to record, to listener and finally to players trying to reproduce the original sound. For this reason, any example of an ethnic music played needs to be completely authentic so that the best model is presented to the children. Someone playing the music of Glenn Miller on a theatre organ will do little to evoke a feeling for life in the 1940s, whereas a recording of the organ in the Tower Ballroom, Blackpool, will evoke a strong sense of what seaside entertainment was like years ago.

Distinctions should, therefore, be made between recordings of authentic performances of pieces of music and those clearly not in the original style. For example, children should be able to see that while Asian pop and film music often employs Western-type orchestras which play the traditional instruments, the performance of a *raga* will include only traditional instruments. In the same way, the classic New Orleans jazz band, which always contains the same instruments, should be distinguished in sound from later jazz bands and orchestras which introduce string and saxophone sections. In that small, earlier group, with its three wind soloists – clarinet, trumpet and trombone – one hears the soprano, tenor and bass voices of the slaves in the plantations. For these people, jazz was a vocal music which accounts for the 'singable' quality of the sounds of these instruments when played in a true style. The success of the 'blues' has its roots in the condition of slavery, and the desperate situation of many of the slaves who, having been liberated, had great difficulty in finding work and drifted to the cities. Here many of them utilised skills which had been built up as pastimes on the plantations – the ability to improvise music and to entertain. The difference between traditional and commercial styles can be recognised.

Recognising sound qualities in instruments

'Pupils should learn to distinguish the sounds made by a range of instruments, individually and in combination' [KS2, AT2, PoS (ii)].

Individual instruments should be discussed in terms of their sounds. It is irrelevant that the oboe has a double reed, the clarinet a single reed and the flute no reed at all. It is far more valuable to encourage children to think of words to describe the sound of an oboe – spooky, old, crackly and sharp have all been offered. How does it compare with the sound of the flute (silvery, smooth, clear, high)? Such definitions may not be generally agreed, but they are the products of considered listening and it is this which is more important than established facts and opinions which some children have been encouraged to learn. There are many pieces of music, ranging from *Tubby the*

Tuba to *Peter and the Wolf* by Prokofiev, which attempt to encourage children to listen to individual sounds. These tend to ascribe qualities to instruments which may not be shared by children, but they can be useful if not forced on children many of whom will not be ready to receive them. The most important thing is that discussion of music must start with the words which children attach to it and that these can, if necessary, be later linked to factual matters which need to be established. Thus, if music for a dance or dramatic situations is to be used, it will be good for children to listen to a number of pieces of approximately the required mood, and to justify their choice. In this activity there is a real reason for listening, without which there is little point in the exercise.

Bands
Military bands

The brass band and the military band can be distinguished by sound. The military band contains both brass and woodwind instruments, and was brought into use mainly to enable marching soldiers to keep in step. It is frequently seen in the United States of America where it is called a 'marching band' and often accompanies college football teams and their cheer leaders to important matches.

In Britain one associates military bands with regiments of the British Army, and they too are often seen performing at half time at football matches as well as at their more usual ceremonial duties.

Brass bands

The brass band, as its name suggests, is comprised purely of brass instruments. The link between the brass band and centres of heavy industry and mining is part of English social history. Before the industrial revolution, playing stringed instruments was a fairly common English pastime. However, as the population moved from agricultural pursuits to the centres of industry, brass instruments began to grow in popularity. Large companies provided sets of instruments and ran their own bands and the tradition of competitive playing was established.

Compare the sounds of a regimental military band and a brass band. The military band is mainly an outdoor ensemble. There are several drummers, and the tone of the trumpets is stronger and designed to carry over a distance. The brass band, on the other hand, has only a single drummer and the tone of the cornets is softer and sweeter and more suited to playing in a hall.

Good examples for listening purposes are

freely available on records, tapes and compact discs. In the field of brass band music one could not do better than to choose recordings by the bands of Grimethorpe Colliery or the Black Dyke Mills, while the Guards regiments, the Central Band of the Royal Air Force or the Marines have recorded much excellent military band music. One of the finest concert (military) bands in the world is the Eastman Rochester band from America which has recorded a wide range of music.

Scottish pipe bands

Another kind of outdoor marching band of a particular distinctive kind is the Scottish pipe band. The Scottish bagpipe has quite a distinctive sound when, for instance, compared with the Cumbrian pipes. The Cumbrian pipes are a solo instrument, and although the Scottish pipes can be played solo, as in a 'lament', a slow, sad piece, they are most usually heard massed.

Steel bands

A useful comparison can be made between the sound of the steel band of the West Indies and the Gamelan of Indonesia. Encourage discussion about the qualities of each ensemble and comparisons between the mellow sounds of the gamelan gongs and the strident quality of the West Indian steel pans which are, traditionally, made from oil drums. Whereas the West Indian instruments are of very recent origin, the gamelan is a very ancient instrument and plays melodies based upon traditional scales. The steel band, however, plays melodies to which words can be sung. The contrast between the two can provide interesting discussion.

The symphony orchestra

There was a time when no school was without its wall charts of 'The Instruments of the Orchestra'. While we cannot expect every child to be taught the instrumental sections of the classical symphony orchestra and to be able to recognise the sounds made by individual instruments, the opportunity to hear a full orchestra live ought to be provided for every child at least once in his lifetime. Preparation needs to be made if a visit is to be arranged and it is hoped that a concert, tailored to the needs of children, can occasionally be made available. Before such a visit the instrumental families of the orchestra (ie. strings, woodwind, brass and percussion) can be discussed, so that, hopefully, the children will have some understanding of what they see and hear.

Britten's *Young Person's Guide to the Orchestra* is particularly useful. In this piece the whole orchestra is shown off, as single instruments, as orchestral sections and finally with the whole group coming together in a tremendous climax. The sound of a large orchestra in a big hall is quite unlike anything which can be produced from a recording. The effect of a concert can be seen in the subsequent writing and art work with which the visit needs to be followed up.

Chapter 9
Playing and singing

'Pupils should memorise and internalise songs and musical ideas of increasing length and/or complexity' [KS2, AT1, PoS (i)].

In moments of unselfconscious music-making, such as sing-songs on coaches, people who do not generally regard themselves as 'musical' often take part in the invention and performance of accompanying rhythm and harmony.

To be able to react naturally to a social music situation and to reply to the demand 'What rhythm shall we clap with this tune?' are two different things.

It is, therefore, helpful to try to ensure that singing and playing in the classroom have the feeling of sociable and almost involuntary activities. It is hoped that this will lead to purposeful singing and playing in smaller, self-organising groups when social skills and self-control will be all important. Confidence gained in unpressured situations will enhance children's performance on more formal occasions and it is likely that, by this means, more will discover the enjoyment of singing and playing, and be prepared to take part.

Above all, the children should feel that the activity is fun. The activities described in this chapter are relevant throughout most of the primary age range, but it is felt that in the nursery and reception years the emphasis must be on the building up of vocal skills using suitable and well-tried materials. Later, children should be encouraged to see how the kinds of activities described in Chapter 4 in which words taken from a rhyme can be turned into accompanying rhythms, can be used in connection with songs.

Suitable classroom instruments

'Pupils should perform pieces/ accompaniments on a widening range of more sophisticated instruments, with increasing dexterity and control of sound' [KS2, AT1, PoS (iv)].

The instruments you choose will often depend upon the size of the children's hands. It was mentioned in Chapter 4 that the 'internal' rhythm provided by the use of word rhythms helps to guide the less easily controllable extremities of the body. In the early stages children find hands difficult to control, so the use of beaters can only compound the difficulty. The types of beater to be employed should therefore be considered very carefully (see Chapter 4, page 31).

There are a number of instruments which are seen in every school's stock, and many of these are, depending upon their quality, entirely satisfactory.

Unpitched instruments

Drums

Most drums are valuable, though it is sometimes desirable to have some kind of stand or to have drums which are self-supporting so that they can be played more easily.

Tambourine

The tambourine is probably the most widely distributed instrument and it is certainly highly versatile and possesses many possible voices. The thing to remember about the tambourine is that it has a 'thumb hole', which is often ignored. The thumb hole enables the instrument to be shaken with a twisting motion, and in this way the sound can be controlled. At the same time, the hole enables the instrument to be held still while the player hits it with the other hand when a rhythmic effect is required.

Children often attempt to play rhythmically by shaking, but this merely produces a blurred sound in the vicinity of the beat. They sometimes also tend to use a clapping motion in which the tambourine and the striking hand are brought towards each other. This results in inaccurate rhythm, particularly when playing quietly, and children should be encouraged to use a technique which most easily produces the desired and accurate effect. This involves holding the instrument still with the skin uppermost, and playing by moving only the other hand.

Wood blocks

Wood blocks played with a hand beater are very useful and seem to invite the proper playing technique, which is similar to that mentioned for the tambourine. The immediacy of their response when struck makes them an ideal school instrument and they should be part of every school's stock.

Claves

Claves and their cheap alternative, the rhythm sticks, are similarly useful. It should be pointed out, however, that one is to be held still while the other is used as a beater. Note, too, that the practice of gripping the more expensive claves, which have a metal-like resonance, is destructive of their tone. Claves should be held lightly between the thumb and fingers and this applies also to rhythm sticks, although the tonal benefit is less noticeable.

Indian bells

Indian bells are a delightful addition to the music stock, though they are often misused. They resemble two tiny cymbals joined together with a piece of tape. One of the discs is tuned slightly sharp (higher in pitch) in relation to the other, so that when they are tapped together a shimmering sound is produced. The correct playing technique is to hold the string in each hand close behind each bell and to use one to strike the other. One often sees children trying to play a sound accurately while seeming to play a solo game of conkers with both bells dangling. Quick notes should not be attempted since the only point of Indian bells is the production of that magical and sustained shimmering tone. Hits in quick succession merely produce the sound of two six-inch nails being hit together which is rather a waste of resources. Two six-inch nails are, however, a useful addition to the instrument stock and are used much the same as rhythm sticks or as beaters for triangles. Take care to blunt their ends!

Maracas

Maracas can play only the rhythms for which they are designed. One on its own is useless, though children can often be seen trying to play a one-handed rhythmic part. As a source for a steady sound in the hands of an inexperienced player, maracas are ineffectual. The sound arrives late and is not encouraging to a child who is trying to play in time. When some experience of the ethnic background of the instrument and some playing technique have been

developed so that the hand movement anticipates the sound, maracas can come into their own. They are, of course, useful as effects instruments, that is, non-rhythmic sound sources. A common rhythm suitable for the instrument is as follows. The capital letter indicates a heavier stroke (R=right and l=left). Try it and see for yourself that the technique needs some practice:

R l l R l l R l (repeated ad lib)

Cymbals

Cymbals are common, though the cheap kind are of little value. Any of less than eight inches in diameter are of little use, since the glory of cymbals is the sustained sound which follows the beater stroke or the clash. Well-made cymbals are, unfortunately, very expensive and the largest prohibitively so. The large single cymbal should never be struck with a metal beater and only rarely with a wooden stick. A soft-headed beater will produce the best effect and prolong the life of an expensive item. A safe storage place should be reserved for the cymbal: it must not be left carelessly in an instrument trolley where other items may be piled on top of it.

Castanets

Castanets of the true Spanish variety are practically useless in school. The playing technique is extremely difficult and is not managed satisfactorily by any but those with a practical skill in Spanish traditional music.

Triangles

Triangles of different sizes should be suspended from proper holders (holding rods with a loop of string on the end) or a loop of thick, stiff cord. Cotton is sometimes used, but the instrument tends to rotate as soon as it has been struck. Try to use a variety of sizes.

Jingles

When shaken, jingles do not play rhythmic patterns too easily except those which have the evenness of the trotting of a horse. A varied rhythm can be played by striking the instrument with the non-holding hand.

Pitched instruments

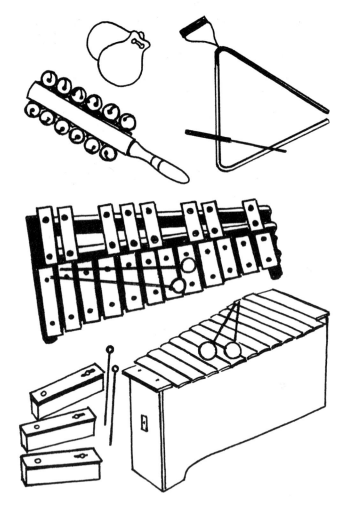

Glockenspiels and chime bars

Glockenspiels and chime bars should not be purchased unless the sound after striking contines for more than one second. There are miniature versions suitable for personal use, but their sound does not carry in the classroom space and this encourages the player to hammer in an attempt to produce an acceptable volume. If better quality instruments are being used at the same time, the sounds made by the miniature instrument become obscured. Soft-headed rubber beaters should be used in preference to the harder plastic and wooden beaters. One or two harder beaters are useful for the production of special effects, but for the general purposes of music-making, the softer variety are generally more useful. Children should be encouraged to let the 'ball' (beater head) bounce to avoid the dampening effect.

Chime bars should always be stored upright in a proper box and never in a heap. Glockenspiels should not be piled up during storage. This avoids the crushing of the rubbers which allow the bars to vibrate cleanly. The three sizes of glockenspiel most often used are soprano, alto and tenor. These are found in two varieties, one with all the sharps and flats included like the piano keyboard (chromatic) and the other having merely the scale of C (diatonic). To the diatonic instrument is added spare F#'s and B♭'s so that notes can be changed. This means that the instrument can be used in more keys instead of just the key of C.

Xylophone

This instrument is very expensive and should be looked after with great care. A variety of beaters need to be available, but soft-headed felt beaters are the best for general use. There are four sizes of xylophone generally available: soprano, alto, tenor and bass. These can be either chromatic or diatonic with extra bars for F#'s and B♭'s.

Sensitivity in playing

It is important, when using any of these instruments, that sensitivity in playing is encouraged and this should be made clear to the children. Generally, the bigger the instrument, the greater the incentive for children to 'bash' it, so when instruments and voices are put together it is best to choose a limited number of the more discrete sounding instruments in order to achieve a balanced sound. Children should be encouraged to evaluate this aspect of their playing, both in the choice of instruments and the way that they are played.

Setting up rhythmic accompaniments

Having ensured that the instruments and their beaters are suitable for the use to which they are to be put, a start can be made in developing rhythmic accompaniments to songs.

Let's take 'Old Macdonald' because it is one of the best known of all songs and can be used with any age range. Build up a rhythmic sequence to be progressively spoken, spoken and clapped, spoken and played and finally played only on classroom instruments. This could take the following format:

Old Macdonald, Old Macdonald (*repeated several times*)
Had a farm, had a farm (*repeated several times*)

Let the whole class speak the first line a number of times. Give the rhythm time to

settle and then begin to clap, encouraging the children to join in. Again, let the rhythm settle, then place your finger on your lips, thus indicating that the class should stop saying the rhythm and just clap. Listen carefully, showing that you are doing so and registering the appropriate reaction to the accuracy of their work.

Make a brisk signal to encourage all the children to stop together; if they don't then try again. Make it clear that neat and accurate performance is required and look round suspiciously to find who forgot to stop.

Work through the rest of the rhyme in the same way, then divide the class in half and let each half practise one of the word rhythms in exactly the same way as was done before.

Now start one half saying, 'Old Macdonald, Old Macdonald', then start the other half saying, 'Had a farm, had a farm'. Signal the children to start clapping and when the rhythm has settled, signal for them to stop saying the words.

Listen attentively, beating time with your hand and then make your signal for them to stop together. If they don't, then try again.

Try to inject punch into this activity and encourage each team to work hard so as to get it right and not let the side down. A third part can be practised in the same way, dividing the class into three, but you must decide whether the children will be capable of this. It may be that just one rhythm needs to played with the verse at first, then two or three depending on success.

Now let the children practise the song with half the class playing the rhythm on instruments, while the other half sing. Reverse the positions so that the players sing and the singers play.

A variation of this activity is as follows: Divide the class into two or three sections then set out two or three groups of instruments in front of the class, for example two drums, two wood blocks and two tambourines. Choose two children from each section to stand at the front of their groups holding the instruments. As before, start one section speaking the words of a song, progress to clapping the beat and indicate when the instrumentalists are to join in. Start the next section in the same way, and then the third. When the whole performance is secure, signal to stop all except the instrumental players and let the whole class sing the song through a couple of times. Change the players and repeat the activity.

The aim of this kind of lesson is to provide a busy and cheerful atmosphere in which a great deal of non-stop rhythmic practice is taken, everyone sings and the idea of making up accompanying rhythms is established.

Singing

'Pupils should sing an expanding repertoire of songs (unison and simple two-part), and pieces requiring a variety of vocal techniques, with increasing understanding and control of pitch, duration, dynamics, diction and phrasing' [KS2, AT1, PoS (iii)].

In the reception year children are gathered together regularly to see things, to talk and to discuss, to listen and, it is hoped, to sing. None of these activities happens in a formal sort of way. If there is time after a lesson ends before lunch, a short poem may be read, discusson of an object of interest may take place or a song may be sung.

The singing may well not be very much in tune and some of it will more resemble enthusiastic shouting, but there will be an acceptance by the children that singing is something that happens naturally and unselfconsciously. Chapter 5, 'Vocal skills', offers solutions to the problems of children who are 'growlers' and who seem unable to sing melodies in tune, but if songs are sung regularly and at a suitable pitch, the necessary remedial work will be kept to a minimum. The less experienced teacher

should not despair at the depressing sound which, at first, meets her ears. She should sing on, giving the best example of which she is capable.

More complex songs

The simple pitching games and easily memorable songs which will have been sung at the beginning of Key Stage One should have enabled children to gain control of their vocal cords and introduced them to an enjoyable activity. During the first three years at school the restricted vocal range of songs at first chosen should be extended so that, as higher notes are able to be reached, more challenging material can be attempted.

This challenge often comes in songs that contain longer notes and phrases than hitherto so that the note being sung has to be controlled with a steady flow of breath. The signature tune to the television programme 'Neighbours' makes some demands of this kind as do many folk songs, such as 'Blow the wind southerly'. There is always a place for shouty fun songs, but vocal skills will not improve if they are the sole diet.

Leaps of an octave can be included as in the round 'Old Abram Brown' by Benjamin Britten. There is in this piece, though, the simplest of melodies, the opportunity for characterism and mock solemnity, and considerable control is necessary to bring it off.

Once children can produce a firm tone, more exciting rhythms can be attempted, and the ability to learn a number of verses provides the opportunity for different treatments of individual verses to be attempted.

There are a number of pairs of songs which can be sung concurrently and produce a very pleasant effect. This is a good method of enjoying two-part singing; teach 'Bobby Shaftoe' and 'Skip to my Lou' and when they are well learned, try them together.

Good vocal sound

Songs like 'Old Macdonald' are not especially helpful for encouraging good singing tone. Indeed, many fun songs are of a 'shouty' character. Choice of songs of a smooth character needs to be made for work in this area and folk and traditional songs are generally suitable. It is a good strategy to ask the children to hum and to sing melodies to 'Aah' and 'Ooh' and to insist upon breathing at the right place. To help the children develop their vocal control, there are certain considerations which can be borne in mind.

Breathing

In the early stages, it is unwise to ask the children to 'take a nice big breath'. With typical child-like gusto, they are likely to take a great gulp of air to their point of bursting and, feeling extremely uncomfortable, they will be in no condition to sing. It is better simply to tell them where to take breaths and to observe them closely to see that they are all able to follow that instruction. As time goes on longer gaps can be requested and a real 'legato line' (smooth flow of melody) will be obtained. Indicate an indrawn breath where it is required by some suitable signal; an upturned hand and opened mouth seems to work well.

Dynamics

The control of dynamics (variations in volume) may have been practised in activities such as the 'Hot and cold game' (Chapter 3, 'Developing listening skills'), but is principally of importance as an element in an interesting performance. Control of dynamics in singing should be developed during the course of Key Stage One and should have reached a good standard in Key Stage Two when dynamic markings as well as breathing instructions expressed in conventional musical terms should be recognised. The conductor's hand expresses loudness or softness by the size of the time-keeping gesture and children soon learn to respond; if they have the good fortune to go to a concert they will see how the conductor manages the matter and they should be encouraged to use the technique in their own directing activities.

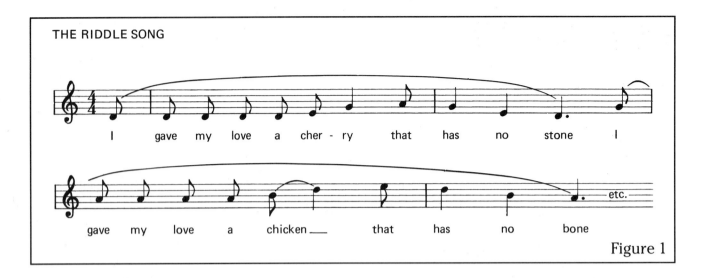

THE RIDDLE SONG

I gave my love a cher-ry that has no stone I
gave my love a chicken that has no bone etc.

Figure 1

When songs have been learned from memory it is all too easy for slackness to creep into the performance. Sustained notes, particularly at the ends of phrases, tend to be cut off leaving an ugly gap in the musical line. Children should be encouraged from the outset to give the longer notes their full value:

Three men went to mo........w

By sustaining the note correctly the intonation (singing in tune) will improve because it is easier to stay in tune while sustaining a note than when, having stopped, one has to start again.

Diction

Clarity of words should always be requested and is not difficult to obtain. It is sometimes sufficient merely to ask for clear words, but one can stop the singing and get the children to speak the words as clearly as possible, really using their lips, teeth and tongues. If this ploy is used regularly, it not only exercises the vocal equipment which produces good diction, but helps to keep the need for it in mind.

Phrasing

Phrasing has very much to do with breathing. A phrase is a complete section of a melody which clearly has a beginning

and an end so that it is an entity and not merely 'a few notes from the tune', as in Figure 1.

Because a melody is made up of phrases, children should be encouraged to 'sing through' each phrase, making it sound like a single component of the melody and not just a length of music made up of separate sounds.

Words relate very much to the phrasing of a song and the natural places in a rhyme where one would take a breath are very often those where a phrase ends and the next begins:

Over the hills and over the sea; (breath)

Swallows of summertime, fly to me.

It hardly matters how naturally good children's voices may have become. Without good diction and phrasing and without proper control of breathing a performance will seem very ordinary. But it is not only the audience who notice. Children themselves soon become aware of the quality of their own performance and derive much satisfaction from doing the job properly.

Chapter 10
Using rounds

'Pupils should maintain a part as a member of a group in a round or simple part song' [KS2, AT1, PoS (v)].

Rounds are an excellent means of producing an impressive choral effect which is enjoyed by both singers and their audience. Composers great and small have composed rounds, ranging from the familiar 'I hear thunder' and 'Three blind mice' to pieces of incredible beauty and complexity by Mozart.

Rounds are easy to use providing that the teacher knows the round by heart and that the children realise that they must wait until it is time for their group to begin. If you don't read music but like the look or sound of a new round, get your music co-ordinator to sing it on to a tape so that you can learn it because it is impossible to teach a round properly with your nose in a book. Rounds are a splendid form of musical co-operation for a class, but the teacher needs to be in full control of the situation.

A class, in whatever year of the primary school, which can sing a clear and pleasant vocal line, may not yet have achieved 'round readiness' and there are certain matters which need to be understood by both teacher and class before rounds can be included in the song repertoire. The first consideration is one of management and the arrangement of singers.

Avoiding common problems

It is tempting to divide the class into two, three or four clearly separated groups. Round singing has been witnessed in a school hall when the four groups were put in the four corners of the room and given names North, South, East and West – as if divided into teams. The effect of this was to create a desire to conquer other teams by singing (shouting) more loudly, and the whole effect was one of vocal warfare. By emphasising the divisions of the choir in this way, the real aim – unity – was lost, so it is advisable to adopt some sort of strategy which maintains the feeling of group co-operation. A suggested method by which this can be achieved is as follows.

Teach the melody to the whole group in one piece, singing it through yourself and encouraging the class to join in as they begin to learn it. Make frequent repetitions and as the class, and then perhaps sections of the class, begin to manage on their own, withdraw your help by singing more and more softly. When the children are able to sing strongly without help, begin to sing the second part yourself, providing a stronger and stronger line. If, at this point, the class becomes confused by the presence of the second part, sing more softly or reinforce the line that the children are singing so that the moment when they *can* sustain their line against another part becomes naturally obvious.

At this point it might be useful to get the class to hum the melody. This establishes the feeling that the round is not to be sung in an aggressive way, and when this is achieved, the class can be divided and the first two-part attempt made using humming. An instruction to hum the tune once and then to use the words will automatically produce a controlled sound and, most importantly, the children will be able to enjoy the effect of two-part singing simply because they will be able to *hear* the effect. Division into three and four parts can follow.

Too often, however, children in other groups begin to sing with the group which is supposed to start instead of awaiting their turn or, when their turn arrives, join in with the stage of the tune being sung by those who started.

One teacher taught the concept of waiting one's turn with an activity at the end of a PE lesson. A round with four parts was chosen (Figure 1) and the children lined up in four 'trains' facing down the length of the hall. After being given the starting note, train one began to sing, walking to the steady rhythm of the music. As the first group reached Point 2 (the first note of the third bar), the second group began to walk to the rhythm of the music, singing as they went. When the first group reached the word 'Pee-wit', the third group began to walk and to sing from the beginning, and at Point 4 the fourth group set out. When the first group reached the end of their verse, they stopped walking and as each succeeding 'train' finished their verse, they also halted. A perfect performance resulted in the four lines of children coming to a halt exactly level with

On the moor I saw a plo-ver, and a cur-lew called her lov-er: Pee - wit, Pee - wit; spring has sure-ly come a-gain.

Figure 1

Figure 2

each other, and considerable satisfaction was registered when the whole operation was perfectly managed.

Sometimes the teacher would ask the children to sing two verses and the four lines would have to sing the round through twice before coming to rest. Upon reaching the end of the hall the leaders of the lines would turn and retrace their steps through the ranks in a 'counter marching' manoeuvre worthy of a military band. However hot the pace of the preceding PE lesson, this procedure had the effect of 'cooling down' the class so that their departure from the hall was quiet and well ordered. The lesson about round singing seemed also to have been learned and, without saying much about it, the teacher had avoided the problem of groups not waiting their turn to begin singing or joining in at the beginning.

Adding instruments to a round

Pupils should **'Play an individual instrumental part in a group piece'** [KS2, AT1, PoS (vi)].

The use of pitched instruments (glockenspiels, chime bars, xylophones, etc) is most effective in the accompaniment of rounds and the provision of the necessary notes is a simple matter.

A round is divided into a number of sections, each of which harmonises with each and all of the rest. When all the parts have joined in, the effect is of each section being sung over and over again at the same time, though by different groups. If, therefore, one instrument plays the first section repeatedly and another plays the second section in the same way, harmonies, which will accompany the melody, will be produced. If all the sections of the round are repeated by different instruments, then a full sounding accompaniment will be produced which makes a very satisfactory classroom orchestral sound. 'London's burning' is one of the best known rounds and is illustrated in Figure 2.

By chopping the melody of the round into its four sections, accompanying parts can be played as in Figure 3.

Glockenspiel 1

Section 1

Glockenspiel 2

Section 2

Xylophone

Section 3

Chime Bars

Section 4

Figure 3

To put the whole piece together, one instrument begins to play a section of the round and is joined by the others in turn. To this can be added unpitched instruments playing word rhythms, and when all are playing, the voices begin. When the round has been sung through as many times as is required, the instruments can stop playing one after the other or as arranged.

Why do rounds 'work'?

When students of music begin to consider the problems facing the composer of a round, the fact that all parts of the tune lock together harmonically seems nothing short of a miracle. If one tries to write two bars of a tune which harmonise with the next two bars and all subsequent two bar sections following, which must also harmonise with each other, it does seem difficult. In fact, the process of writing a round is much more simple than one might think. If a chord sequence corresponding in length to the sections of the round is borne in mind, and the sections of melody made to harmonise with it, each section will automatically accompany each and every other section.

Composing rounds in the classroom

Give separate groups of children a sequence of guitar chords and ask them to improvise melodies over it. If the melodies fit the chord sequence, their tunes will harmonise. Refer to the chart on page 114 for an explanation of guitar chords.

When Mozart wrote his Italian 'Love poem' rounds, one of which is for four four-part choirs, he concealed this structure as one might expect of a composer of his greatness. The structure is, however, there, as is the harmonic structure of 'Three blind mice'. In this nursery rhyme, the composer makes little attempt to hide his methods. The chord sequence C, G7, C is repeated eight times with a one-beat rest after the third chord:

C,   G,   C,   –,
1   2   3   4
C,   G7,   C,   –,
1   2   3   4 etc.

Let a group of children play one of the shorter specimen chord sequences shown in Chapter 20 (page 178) four times, and ask another group to make up a tune to go with it. This will work as a round. The following example was the work of four Y5

children, who continued to work on their round at playtimes and odd moments. The words were lines from the Flanders and Swann song about the weather:

In July the sun is hot,
Is it shining? No it's not!

This was the chosen chord sequence:

D, Bm, G, A

The sequence was played over and over again and different tunes tried on the glockenspiel. There was a problem about writing it down as no one had a good enough grasp of standard musical notation to use this system; the method adopted was as shown in Figure 4.

d	e	f#	d	e	d	c#	–
f#	e	f#	d	g	f#	e	–
a	a	b	b	b	d	c#	–
d	a	b	d	b	g	a	–

Figure 4

The teacher wrote it out in standard notation (Figure 5) and recorder players were imported to help try it out. After the first performance there were a few furrowed brows and unappreciative noises and a deputation arrived at the staff room door: 'It doesn't work, Sir'.

'Sir' suggested that they mark on the music the places where it 'didn't work' and, after some encouragement, improvements were made and the final version performed at an assembly with the whole class either playing or singing.

It is good for children to experience the difficulties which they have made for themselves and to correct their own work. If notes have been included which are beyond singable vocal range, then they will have to change them. Their choice of chord sequence, or better still their own choice of chords, their choice of words and their having to wrestle with practicalities all provide an excellent parallel to work in technology. They will have identified a need, selected materials and tried to find ways in which these can be fitted together. The test of the prototype is always followed by alterations to the design and more tests then take place. It is often likely that more performers will need to be provided to achieve the intended outcome and decisions about what extra skills are required will have to be made – an exercise in problem-solving of which any class could be proud.

Sensitivity in performance

When a round is well known, it is an excellent vehicle for the practice of varied and sensitive singing. Depending upon the mood of the music and words, discussion of how the round is to be performed needs to take place.

'O, how lovely is the evening
When the bells are sweetly ringing,
Ding dong, ding dong, ding dong'

This round may suggest a soft, sweet first verse, leading to a gentle crescendo the next time round with strong bell effects. The third time through starts strongly but

Figure 5

begins to grow softer so that as the voices stop, an impression of the setting sun is produced. This effect could have been expressed in a variety of media, but in this case it has to be done purely by tone of voice and thus presents a considerable imaginative challenge.

Massed singing

One good reason for an assembly is that it gives the school an opportunity to gather together as one single family. Appropriate prayers may be said, work shown for corporate approval and matters of general interest and management stated. Singing by the whole school has a good effect in drawing the whole community together, and the use of a well-known round provides an exciting and challenging musical exercise. The teachers need to join in this exercise, indicating to their class when to start. With the addition of whatever instrumental players are available, the whole effect can be very pleasing.

Few people realise that 'The first nowell', the well-known Christmas carol, can be performed as a round. At the end of a Christmas concert the entire cast and audience can take part. If a short rehearsal for the mums and dads can be arranged before the concert begins, and if a member of staff is delegated to start them at the right moment, the unifying effect at a celebration of the great family festival can be very powerful, not to say moving. Massed choral singing can be a thrilling experience for children – to sing in parts is even more so and for this reason the use of rounds should be encouraged in festivals great and small.

Any song, written using the pentatonic scale (see Chapter 11), will work as a round and there are many excellent books available which provide useful repertoires at a variety of levels. These often state the age range for which their contents are intended but, as has been emphasised, round-readiness has to be built up. When this is achieved the effort in doing so will be well worth it.

Chapter 11
Developing composition skills

Pupils should **'Devise and develop musical ideas within simple structures'** [KS2, AT1 (d)].

A variety of styles

If a young child is asked to paint a picture, he will most likely choose 'My mum', or 'A fire engine'. He will not usually decide to paint 'My hot picture', or any other title which implies thinking of graphic art as a means of communicating abstract ideas and not just as a kind of inaccurate photograph. In the same way, a child who

is asked to compose music will most likely think that she has to make up a tune unless she has been introduced to wider possibilities. These include the portrayals of mood and impression which do not necessarily involve the use of melody. Like a formal technique in graphic art, using melody requires some experience. A natural freedom exists in impressionistic composition in an art form, which is encouraging to people of any age who are, for the first time, experiencing its use.

When children begin to use music as communication, to compose and to perform, the element of exploration must

be a central consideration. Reception children usually have little skill in music, though a great deal of curiosity, so activities leading to an impressionistic style of composition seem an appropriate approach to their music-making. This approach should be continued throughout their time at school, though it is not simply an easy way out which avoids the need for knowledge of the system of music which has been our Western cultural heritage for at least 400 years.

Modern music uses sounds which may, to many, seem as if they are randomly chosen, although they are actually very carefully ordered by the composer. It may be that because such music cannot definitely be said to be 'wrong' – because few are sufficiently familiar with the style to judge – that this method of composition is used exclusively in some schools.

The difference between these two kinds of composition is simply that conventional music has, in the West, developed over hundreds of years and, because of its

historical development, listeners are able to know what to expect. Music in a free impressionistic style owes no relationship to any particular heritage and cannot, consequently, be judged by the same criteria. This is not to say, however, that aesthetic judgements cannot be made about either style of music.

While there is great value in using impressionistic composition in education at any age range, there is no reason why conventional sounds should not also be introduced into class compositions at the primary level. Gillian, Y5, once asked, 'Sir, how do you make proper music, like for the piano and all that?' She explained that you never heard on the radio the kind of music we had been working on (she has obviously never heard of Radio 3) and said that we ought to do some. She had taken part in the piece referred to in Chapter 6 (page 45), in which the players had walked about and, while enthusiastic and reasonable, she rightly suspected that her teacher was not laying the whole world at her feet.

Her class had worked on the provision of rhythmic and pitched accompaniments to known rhymes and songs and had played the chords indicated for guitar players (Chapter 15). They had sung rounds and added instrumental parts to them, but they had not yet had control of something for which Gillian did not know the name, though she suspected that it was there. What she wanted to be able to use in composing was harmony.

The importance of aural experience

In the past, harmony was written by the majority of students working towards exams using a sort of sum which had rigid rules as to how it was to be solved. This is the way in which thousands were successful in 'O' level mathematics; by knowing how to solve the equation without the slightest inkling of how it applied to real life. What was often lacking was the ability to hear what they needed to write down because the system of teaching often did not provide this experience. Traditional Western harmony is comprehended in the brain only through experience of the ear, so that to be able to compose and organise harmony for people to play, one must have an aural imagination which can envisage what instructions need to be given to the player. Experience does not necessarily have to involve specialist terms. It is essential and is not as difficult to provide as it may seem.

First, however, it is important to reassure children that they can put together sounds which seem acceptable. A good approach is to use the pentatonic scale because there is no chance of the result sounding 'wrong'. This is because none of the notes of the pentatonic scale clashes with any other because the scale contains no semitones, that is, adjacent notes.

Using the pentatonic scale

Depending upon the experience of the children, this kind of work can be started simply in Y3 or Y4. It is best begun with improvising using the pentatonic scale so that the idea of 'busking' (making music up on the spot) to an accompaniment can be experienced.

A pentatonic scale can be formed on any note and can be most clearly demonstrated using a glockenspiel or a piano.

The seven white notes are as follows and may be numbered:

C D E F G A B
1 2 3 4 5 6 7

This scale above is commonly expressed in tonic sol-fa notation as the 'doh, re, me, fa, soh, la, ti, doh' scale which is called the diatonic scale.

The five pentatonic scale notes are:

1 2 3 5 6

The pentatonic scale on C is therefore:

C D E G A

These notes can be played together in any combination at random which produces a rather pleasant Chinese-sounding concoction. Although most people identify the sound as Chinese, it may be noted that many Scottish airs, for example 'Auld lang syne', use this scale for their melody and that it is built into the national instrument of that nation – Scottish bagpipes. Extensive use of the pentatonic scale was also made by French impressionist composers at the beginning of the twentieth century, so the pentatonic scale is not a mere classroom device. In fact, the pan pipe carved on an Ancient Greek marble in the British Museum would have sounded the notes of the pentatonic scale, so it is clear that the scale was also used by the Ancient Greeks.

Ask a child to start an ostinato (see Chapter 4) on a glockenspiel, using notes from a pentatonic scale, then let a second child join in with chime bars and make up a different ostinato. Ostinato on drum and wood block can then join in and thus a pentatonic piece can be composed. Figure 1 gives an example.

---

1) Glockenspiel

C   G   A   G/   C   G   A   G/
        (repeat)

2) Chime bars

E   D   C   -/   E   D   C   -/
        (repeat)

3) Drum

*   –   *   */   *   –   *   */
        (repeat)

4) Wood block

x   xx   x   x/   x   xx   x   x/
        (repeat)

Figure 1

When a number of ostinati have been put together in this way, words sung on the pentatonic notes can be added with the help of a glockenspiel. For example:

    Ca-ra-van
    C   D E
    By the sea
    G   A G
    Now it's sum-mer,
    C   D   E   G
    Wait for me.
    E   D   C

As the instruments join in one by one, so they can drop out after the words have been sung however many times the children think necessary. The alternative is for someone to give a signal for everyone to end together.

When this kind of composition has become accepted and children's own words have been used to set to music, a more challenging kind of composition can be attempted.

Composition using chords

Anyone playing or making up music tends to recoil from what they hear as a 'wrong' note, so firmly, if unconsciously, is their taste conditioned by experience of Western musical culture. In using a system which seems to have its 'rights and wrongs', this aesthetic sense is a force which, in improvisation, acts as a teaching influence so that the student moves from recognition of an unsuitable sound to the ability to avoid playing one. Improvisation of a melody against a chord sequence provides this experience. Once children are used to handling instruments and playing with a group, the chords which make up the Western system of harmony may be introduced.

The use of chords can be introduced to the whole class in a teacher-directed lesson. The equipment needed is minimal and most schools are likely to possess what is necessary. The equipment required comprises a glockenspiel, one each of D, E, F, A and B chime bars and two C and G

chime bars. The two C's and two G's don't have to be the same size and pitch. Begin by giving three children bars sounding C, E and G. This group will be known as group C. Let three more have F, A and C (group F) and three others have G, B and D (group G). Explain that the groups are named after the chord which they will play, when directed. For example, when group C play their bars together a chord of C is sounded (CEG). Encourage the others to play a steady rhythm with finger clicks. Let each group play in turn in time with the rhythm.

The sequence can be repeated any number of times with different groups of players. While the rest of the class are awaiting their turn to play the chord sequence they are becoming familiar with the repeated harmony.

The next step is to invite children to take turns in making up a tune on the glockenspiel to fit to the harmony. They will soon get the feeling of what works and what produces a 'clash'.

It may make it easier for the melody players if two soundings of each chord are played by the chime bar players, for example:

C C – F F – G G – C C

If this is played at a steady walking pace and a restricted number of notes on the glockenspiel made available (C D E F G will do for a start), there will not be too many possible unsatisfactory combinations of melody and chord.

The very presence of these possible clashes is, however, useful because if there were a totally bland and acceptable outcome of any combination of notes in this work, then the exercise of preference and choice by the player would not be rewarded; there would, in fact, be no furtherance of learning. It is for this reason that use of the pentatonic scale has its limitations because, as was seen, any combination of notes of that scale is acceptable.

To give the glockenspiel player something to guide her rhythm, use some simple words to shape the rhythm of the tune which will then turn into a song. For example:

O-ver the/hills and/o-ver the/sea,
Swall-ows of/ summertime/fly to/me.

This example allows for two playings of the chord sequence. The words between the divisions (/) correspond with two beats on the chime bars:

C C/ F F/ G G/ C C/ (repeat)

Let the child play her tune through a few times until she decides on a final version, when the rest of the class can sing along.

Once this activity has been understood in principle, continue it as a group activity in which children can take turns in playing the tune. If a number of groups work together, a shortage of instruments may then ensue, but one group working on its own can try out the activity while others are otherwise engaged.

Alternatively, an approach to chord playing which involves fewer players can be initiated. Chapter 15 shows that guitar chords can be transcribed for use with classroom instruments and explains how the chords can be played by three children instead of the ten required above.

Some specimen sequences are also included in the resources section at the end of the book and there are instructions on how children can design their own sets of chords. A specimen sequence might look like this:

1) G F# G F# G F# G G
2) D D D D E D D D
3) B A B A C A B B

1, 2 and 3 are the three players who would try out the sequence to which a tune from the scale supplied would be added: G, A, B, C, D, E, F#, G.

This leads to the children being able, by at least Y6 or Y7, to organise their own chords and to make use of the chord facilities built into electronic keyboards.

Chapter 4 describes how a rhythmic poem can be spoken to the accompaniment

of unpitched rhythm. When that stage has been reached, a melody can be made up for the poem, either using pentatonic notes or the full diatonic scale (doh up to doh).

A diatonic scale can be played starting on any note and some of these and their appropriate chords are contained in the resources section. The 'chord cards' illustrated there can be placed in an order chosen by children and tried out before they add a melody.

Composition using polyrhythms

From the conventional chords of Western harmony we move to a completely different method of composition which may be used simply from Y3 and which, as the range increases, can be allowed to become increasingly complex.

Polyrhythms are great fun and also a considerable test of concentration and rhythmic sense. Intricate compositions and weird and wonderful harmonies can be produced by their use. Clashes and consonances result from a mathematical pattern which can help to explain products.

Get the class to count: 1 2 3, 1 2 3, 1 2 3, etc. This is a counted section of three. Now let them clap on the first beat * 2 3, * 2 3, * 2 3.

Now try: * 2 3 4, * 2 3 4, * 2 3 4. This is a counted section of four.

Divide the class in half. Beat on a drum at a steady pulse to keep them in time. Explain that they will all start together on '1', but one half will clap * 2 3, and the other half will clap * 2 3 4. This will result in claps sounding at different times in relation to each other, sometimes together, sometimes consecutively and sometimes not.

Ask the children to work out how many beats will happen before both halves clap together again (12 because $3 \times 4 = 12$). Is there a pattern (12, 24, 36, 48 etc)?

Divide the class into three groups:

* 2 3
* 2 3 4
* 2 3 4 5

Ask the children again to work out how many claps happen before all clap together ($3 \times 4 \times 5$).

Divide the class into groups of nine or ten so that they can try out polyrhythms on their own. Give one person in each group an instrument such as a drum to keep a steady beat going. Encourage three or four members of each group to make one body sound (a 'pop' made with the finger across the mouth, perhaps?) while another section of the group claps and a third clicks their fingers, all using different repeated number patterns. Oohs and aahs are other possibilities.

Unpitched instruments can also be used and the number of sections within a group varied as required. After a while, make the keeping of a steady beat visual rather than aural, with one member of the group using a pointed finger in a rhythmic conducting exercise. As the children begin to develop an internal rhythm a conductor may be unnecessary, but it all depends upon the needs of the group.

Beating time

The correct method of beating time in various bar lengths may not be essential here, but children enjoy getting such details right and the patterns for two, three and four beats in the bar are shown in Figures 2 to 4. The directions of the beat are shown from the view of the conductor; clearly, the orchestra sees them in the reverse direction!

Polyrhythms and pitched instruments

When the children are sufficiently confident, introduce pitched notes. If there are not enough instruments for each child in the group to have one, let them take turns playing an instrument while the others help them count. Make sure that there is fair distribution of labour!

If, for example, a group of ten children are working together, one option is to give

them C, D, E, F, G – the first five notes of the diatonic scale in the key of C. A second option would be to give them E, C#, D and E flat. These are very close together so they tend to clash and make a much more acidic sound while randomly chosen notes provide infinite variety, especially if unpitched instruments are also included.

The children will gradually realise that by choosing what notes to use, and by adding some unpitched percussion instruments, different moods and effects can be achieved. They may decide to use longer counted sections, such as 6 7 8 and 9, if they get tired of the sound repeated

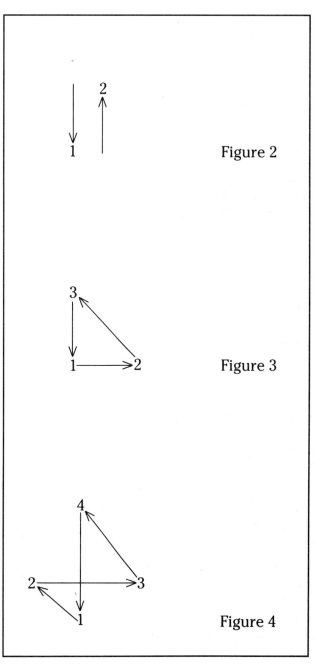

Figure 2

Figure 3

Figure 4

every three counts. The early work seems pedestrian but with experience, considerable variety and expressive quality can be developed.

There is a tendency for children to use the same speed of basic pulse to which polyrhythms are fitted. Emphasise that the more variety in speeds that is used, the greater the variety of moods available. When the children have discovered how to adjust the effect to suit the needs of their work, they will find that this kind of music makes excellent background music to a play or for a dance. For example, the starlight in a nativity play will need a twinkling kind of music, as will the incidental music for a Diwali play. To create the right kind of sound to fit the occasion is an excellent compositional exercise.

Compositional styles

It is hoped that children will reflect upon methods used in the past and decide how moods and effects can be obtained. They may now decide to compose in that free and impressionistic style which was mentioned earlier and include elements of other styles encountered.

There may be a section at the beginning of a piece which uses chords and this may be followed by a pentatonic section after which the first part is played again. This introduces the matter of form which is present in all kinds of music and which should be recognised. Different sections and repeats of those heard earlier were mentioned in Chapter 3, on page 24. Now it is a matter of deciding what 'form' a composition needs to take. Simple A – B – A is just one example, but there are many possibilities and it is good for children both to recognise forms in songs and to decide what they will use in their own compositions.

As time goes on, the choice of sounds, contrasting sections and relationships between them will develop so that the word 'composition' will begin to mean what artists refer to in composition of a picture. Balance and contrast can be discussed and the children will gradually come to experience music as a creative art.

Chapter 12
Performance

Pupils should:
'Share their music-making, presenting their performances effectively to different audiences, for different purposes, and in a number of places with different acoustics' [KS1, AT1, PoS (vi)].

'Plan and present their own projects/ performances, being aware of the need to communicate to different audiences' [KS2, AT1, PoS (viii)].

A child who knows that her work will not be looked at will see no point in bothering to put any effort into its production. Children's work is displayed as a way of saying, 'Thank you. I liked your work and I have taken trouble to make it look nice. I'm looking forward to what you do next!'

There is less chance to give so ephemeral a product as a piece of music, whether composed, learned or improvised, the opportunity to be appreciated than work in almost any other subject area, with the exception of movement. It is, however, essential that all musical work is given this consideration, otherwise the children's motivation will soon dwindle.

Performance in class

An understanding of the disciplines and style required for more formal recitals, such as those in the hall or outside the school, can be gained and should begin by performance in the classroom. Performance invariably provides a satisfactory conclusion to a music lesson.

If, for example, an exercise involving words with a rhythmic accompaniment has been put together, time needs to be allowed for its performance. This should not be merely 'the last try through' but something rather more special and slightly more formal which will help to establish that music is a form of communication.

The audience

A performance, of course, needs an audience. The simplest way of providing that is to use a tape recorder. Record the name of the piece and the date at the outset so that, after days or weeks or months, a comparison can be made and progress and improved skills can be appreciated.

As the children are working on their pieces, emphasise the fact that a recording is to be made and urge them to make the best use of the time available. Ensure that you consider all the small details so that the quality of the piece will be as good as can be.

'When the rhythm sticks start, are they together? Do they manage to grow a little louder before the tambourines come in?' Try to introduce questions such as these when organising the performance and encourage the children to think about them when, with the help of the tape, they become their own audience and evaluate their own work.

In this way, discriminating listening can be encouraged. This will, in turn, have a good effect upon performance disciplines: the knowledge that a performance will be open to reasoned criticism will tend to make the players exercise self-judgement while playing.

The basic discipline of performance is that players should include their audience in what they are doing and, in a way, offer their music to the audience. For performers to mutter among themselves or to giggle and shuffle and face away from the audience will immediately place a barrier between them and the listeners who will soon react by letting their attention wander.

A visitor may be used to act as an audience. The head, the caretaker or a visiting instrumental teacher are all fair game! Such visitors should be provided with a seat while the performers should stand. However, if there is no available audience, merely standing up to perform has, in itself, a feeling of formality. If all else fails, this can provide that extra sense of occasion. 'Now, let's all stand up and play it as well as we can,' gives a satisfactory feeling to a lesson's end. When working in groups with a number of children in a large room, it can be helpful for the audience to leave their seats and to gather round the group which is going to play. This is beneficial as it creates a feeling of 'coming to listen' and the physical effort of doing so concentrates the attention of the listeners. It also puts the players under some slight pressure and encourages them to do their best.

Presentation

Children should be given a few minutes' warning before the group compositions are to be heard. This gives them time to decide exactly how they mean to start and helps to avoid undignified mistakes and consequent argument. As in any performance, they should also be encouraged to think about the best way in which the performance should be communicated to the audience. It is not enough to play their music; it should be presented in a way that is inviting to the listener and allows the performers to be both seen and heard.

'Have you decided how to start and to stop?' should be a regular consideration if the material used is the kind that can continue ad infinitum, such as the pentatonic scale or polyrhythms. (These are composition devices which are explained in Chapter 11.)

'The piece was very good, but the ending still needs some work' or 'I think we would have preferred to see your face instead of your back' are the kinds of comments which help to make children aware of what is needed for a performance. Presentation should be evaluated as being of equal importance to the musical content of a piece.

Evaluation

When the players have finished, evaluation can be encouraged before the children regroup around the next group to play. The fact that there is a session of evaluation after every performance provides a constant reminder that self-assessment and assessment of others' work are natural outcomes of, and reasons for, listening.

Performance at assembly

Performance in front of the rest of the school will be enhanced if the above-mentioned considerations have become second nature. The evaluation process will, on this occasion, take place back in the classroom.

The headteacher has much to do with the mood in which children return to work after an assembly, and an appreciative vote of thanks will do much to leave them with a pleasant memory of the occasion. It is up to the class teacher, however, to see that the performance gets off to a good start.

Stage management

Knowing the words, the music and the movements are important, but the actual content is only part of the story. Good stage management is crucial.

Practise the starting position at rehearsal by arranging the children where they should be and then telling them to look around to see who is next to them and where they are. Ask them to leave the

platform, line up down the side of the hall and then, very quietly, resume their positions. This should be repeated as necessary and note taken of what props and instruments need to be ready. This is an excellent exercise in responsibility. It is worth considering letting the children with a reputation for silly behaviour take charge of something of importance which is exposed to the audience's view. A little responsibility can very often work wonders.

If possible, prepare the hall before the assembly and then return the children to the classroom. Try to arrange it so that the school assembles and then the class taking part walks quietly and purposefully in and takes its place. This will help to establish an excellent atmosphere, and if the action can begin without a break, so much the better.

The teacher's role

Many a performance has been spoiled by the teacher standing between the class and the audience, furiously mouthing words. This immediately suggests to all concerned that the teacher doesn't trust the children to remember the words. This impression

that the children will not manage without the active participation by their teacher can be removed if practice for an assembly is begun well before the event. The idea that a performance will eventually be involved will act as an additional stimulus to the normal curriculum work involved.

Issues concerning stage management and design should be considered concurrently. A hastily prepared theme, unrelated to day-to-day work, is more likely to produce anxiety in all concerned.

Class identity and co-operation

It is important that the children see themselves as a single unit which can co-operate happily in an endeavour. The preparation of an assembly will set the tone for the week, and disciplines of performance and the need to rely upon each other's efforts will provide a valuable and lasting social experience. It is for this reason that gathering together the class at the beginning of a day, so that a specific matter can be considered, pays dividends. This may take the form of some kind of performance or appreciation of work done

90

and is useful in re-establishing the valuable 'whole class' feeling, especially when so much work is done in smaller groups.

A similarly valuable feeling of group responsibility can be generated if, in the preparation of a song, the teacher requires audible words, specific moments when the class must sing softly or loudly and an overall encapsulation of the spirit of the music. The difference between one performance when all the singers seem to be operating as individuals, and another when there is a feeling of oneness, is marked. The class which is used to attending to these musical details will also most likely work together smoothly in other contexts. When the day comes when the children board a bus to visit another school, it is likely that experience of performance in their own school and attention to detail in what they are about to do will set the tone for the whole outing.

Music festivals

District music festivals are often held in school halls and, therefore, because of the space available, only a selected group of children will be able to attend. This is no problem if every child has the option to belong to the choir. The idea of rejecting a child because of present ability is

abhorrent. When volunteers are called for, many children will offer their services for the choir; those who don't at first understand that this is not a soft option will soon drop out. Choirs which are self-selected in this way do just as well as those made up of chosen children.

Rivalry between schools is often unfair, unjust and unnecessary. Of course, healthy competition can exist between properly trained choirs. However, the kinds of festivals which include work done in the music curriculum time in the classroom, and to which all can go, must be purely for making music together and listening to one another.

Some larger festivals take place in city town halls and allow children to experience the thrill of singing with hundreds of other children. At such events they will be rehearsed by an enthusiastic expert and, with luck, be accompanied by a huge youth orchestra. Here the children will experience the excitement of performance, though hardly in the sense which has been discussed. There may be no room for an audience but there will be a sense of singing to each other and of participation in something tremendous.

The excitement of sending one's voice into a resonant acoustic is recognised by children and is a valuable experience. This is obvious in buildings where concerts take

place, but even small children in pushchairs can be heard experimenting in pedestrian underpasses in shopping precincts. This experience clearly produces a thrill which children are quick to notice.

At the district school festivals, when each school takes turns to sing to the rest and also joins in the massed singing, it is good if the singers and players can dress somewhat similarly. There is still much controversy about school uniform, but if everyone wears a white shirt or blouse, this will produce a unifying effect which is important in performance. It has been said that if a choir looks right, it will sound right and this, to an extent, is true.

In addition to the large events, there are also little festivals where, for example, two first schools might take it in turns to visit each other. At such an event the whole of both schools might take part and individual items be performed with great pride while those listening receive the performances with tumultuous approval. There might be a nominal adjudicator whose job is to say how much he enjoyed the singing and to offer praise and encouragement. He is there to provide the dignity with which all performances should be welcomed and it is important that teachers and guests deport themselves in an appropriate manner; children are quick to detect a careless or patronising attitude.

Music as a curriculum subject

Though participation in festivals and concerts, and performances within the school, are common events, the process of developing music as a curriculum subject for all pupils has sometimes been considered less important than the performances which give the school a good name. These events should contain and reflect the real school music: that which is developed within the curriculum. They are then of much greater value, especially to those children who, in a mere public relations exercise, might be excluded. The planning and strategies of curriculum work should not become subservient to the need to give a concert. When this happens it is the apparently less musically gifted who lose the opportunities which should be offered to them.

If one believes that music has value in school, then it is the less obviously gifted who may be said to require the most help. Would one accept a situation in which a child who was weak at maths was excluded because of his low ability? A kindly visitor to a school in London asked a small boy, 'What are you doing in the Christmas concert?' 'I'm not in nuffink,' was the reply: a considerable comment on the system.

Chapter 13
Connections across the curriculum

It would be good if the children for whom mathematics is a total mystery could engage in a musical, artistic or dramatic activity which was able to teach maths from a completely different perspective; it would be equally good if, by mathematical means, a sensitive response to the arts could be developed in children who find artistic matters incomprehensible. None of this is, of course, possible because links and connections can only reinforce existing understanding. These links are nevertheless valuable and real.

There is some value in the casual incorporation of a mathematical or scientific concept into a music lesson, but it is far better to plan such connections into a theme so that the children are encouraged to take a wider and more purposeful view of their work.

Mathematics
Length

In one Y1 class an exercise in sorting things into order of length, which led to a graphical representation of the children's heights, included the use of chime bars. All kinds of objects were sorted, but when the chime bars were used, the children were asked if there was a way in which the order of length could be checked. Two children sorted a selection of bars behind a screen, while the others *listened* to see if the order was correct.

The principle was further checked with a small, home-made set of tubular bells on the sound table. It was noticed that 2 × 5cm strips of pine which had been cut into different lengths would, if held between finger and thumb and struck with a beater, produce a higher or lower resonance. Would it be possible to cut lengths of wood to make the notes required for an instrument like the tubular bells?

Scientific investigation took place with the help of comparison and measurement and, under the supervision of the teacher and with the help of a safety device, the children sawed, drilled and threaded the 'notes' on to string. A piece of wood, half the length of another, was pronounced as 'having the same note only different'; the teacher chose not to complicate the matter by talking about 'octaves'.

Leroy, who had more than once cut too much off his wood, thought that it was better to make the 'big' bars first so that 'you can use them for a smaller bar if it's wrong'. He was barely able to read and flatly refused to write; nevertheless he brought to the testing procedure a critical accuracy and enthusiasm which was good to see. The two instruments thus produced were kept on the sound table, neither in tune with each other nor producing a scale known to any culture so far discovered, nevertheless they represented work which had drawn on several areas of the curriculum.

Patterns

A project on 'patterns' was run in one Y4 class and during that time much excellent work took place across the curriculum. Number bonds and progressions were included as well as the tessellation of shapes. Patterns in poetry were discussed in terms of both mood and balance and the study of the movement of water led to predictions about what would happen to a given size of boat in waves of a controlled size. Boats were built and tested, and music, art, drama and physical education both contributed to and benefited from this common interest. The assembly at which the work was shown was on the subject of co-operation with one's fellow humans and care for the patterns of the living world, and ended with the 'Mexican wave'.

It is tempting to describe all the work that took place in order to show that music was not just 'tacked on', but to do so would be outside the terms of reference of this book. Instead it would be appropriate to show the links between music and the core subjects as they occurred in a pleasing 'two-way traffic'.

Patterns in number

Addition and subtraction facts up to ten were charted on a grid and the pattern observed (Figure 1). Having noted that pairs of numbers made up ten it was found

	1 2 3 4 5 6 7 8 9 10
1+9	✳ △ △ △ △ △ △ △ △
2+8	✳ ✳ △ △ △ △ △ △ △
3+7	✳ ✳ ✳ △ △ △ △ △ △
4+6	✳ ✳ ✳ ✳ △ △ △ △ △

Figure 1

that a composition could be created and the grid used as notation. One pair of children chose the line of three and seven, and with a tambourine and wood block played:

Tambourine Tambourine Tambourine Block Block Block Block Block Block Block

A second pair chose the line of four and six and with claves and a chime bar played:

Claves Claves Claves Claves Chime Chime Chime Chime Chime Chime

Other pairs chose different lines and instruments and, by playing the lines simultaneously, an interesting texture was produced.

This format of the piece only lasted for ten beats, so it was decided the whole grid could be played in the form of a round with the first pair of children beginning at the

94

first line and the second pair beginning at the first line when the first pair reached the second line.

In this way a number of pairs could take part and the musical effect was that of a piece which began with solo instruments, grew and reached a climax in which all were playing and then subsided to a solo ending. It was found that a more interesting texture could be achieved by re-ordering the lines from the initial order of one and nine, two and eight, three and seven etc., and the kind of arrangement shown in Figure 2 was thought by this group to be particularly satisfactory.

```
          1 2 3 4 5 6 7 8 9 10
   5+5  ∗ ∗ ∗ ∗ ∗ ∆ ∆ ∆ ∆ ∆
   8+2  ∗ ∗ ∗ ∗ ∗ ∗ ∗ ∗ ∆ ∆
   3+7  ∗ ∗ ∗ ∆ ∆ ∆ ∆ ∆ ∆ ∆
   1+9  ∗ ∆ ∆ ∆ ∆ ∆ ∆ ∆ ∆ ∆
   4+6  ∗ ∗ ∗ ∗ ∆ ∆ ∆ ∆ ∆ ∆
   2+8  ∗ ∗ ∆ ∆ ∆ ∆ ∆ ∆ ∆ ∆
```

Figure 2

The teacher suggested that this kind of rhythmic notation could be used to accompany a song. She got out her guitar and the group sang 'Froggie was a good man'. They found that something was wrong and that the rhythm didn't fit. The teacher then suggested that they should find out how long the number strips needed to be and left them to work it out, and a pattern within the song was discovered (Figure 3).

```
          1 2 3 4 5 6 7 8
   4+4  ∗ ∗ ∗ ∗ ∆ ∆ ∆ ∆
   6+2  ∗ ∗ ∗ ∗ ∗ ∗ ∆ ∆
   3+5  ∗ ∗ ∗ ∆ ∆ ∆ ∆ ∆
   1+7  ∗ ∆ ∆ ∆ ∆ ∆ ∆ ∆
```

Figure 3

There were too many lines on the grid to fit the song exactly and the 'one plus seven' line was thought boring. The necessary number of lines to fit one verse of the song (four) was agreed upon and the most interesting lines selected as a rhythmic accompaniment. There was much satisfaction when the rhythms ended at the same time as the music of the song. It was suggested that it might work for other songs and 'Donkey riding' was tried out by one group without the help of the teacher, while another worked on 'God has made a wonderful world'.

A day or two later, a song with three beats in the bar (3/4) caused problems but the difference in metre was discovered by some of the children themselves who said, 'In that sort of music you have to hit slower'. For example:

Froggie was a/good man/he did/ride (2/4)
Windy old/weather/stormy old/weather (3/4).

The explanation may not have been strictly accurate but if you clap at the beginning of the bars indicated, you can see what they meant.

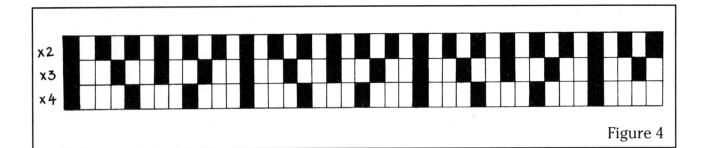

Figure 4

Patterns in multiplication

Number lines had been used to investigate the process of multiplication and coloured paper squares had been gummed on to a large sheet of paper to see what pattern emerged. Twos, threes and fours produced the pattern shown in Figure 4.

The possibilities of using this as a rhythmic pattern were explored and three players of unpitched instruments took a line each and played when the counted pulse reached a blacked-in box. It was found that one did not need to have a long piece of paper to play, though the pattern was then less obvious. The teacher asked how many counts would pass before all the instruments sounded together if a 'five' line was added to the existing three. One group began a lengthy process with graph paper squares, another tried counting while the players played the four lines. After a good deal of 'human error' and consequent frayed tempers, the two groups came to the same conclusion in about the same length of time.

This kind of activity is also discussed in Chapter 11 in the section dealing with 'polyrhythms' (page 84).

Time

Unless children are given the opportunity to experience the passage of periods of time of known duration, they have no means of being able to understand that element which rules all our lives; one more minute in the swimming bath is an instant while a minute standing on one leg is an age. Time is important in music, being related to the ability of sound sources to sustain a note, to the linear quality of music itself and to the equal sections which are so much part of the Western tradition.

The comparison of the lengths of time during which two instruments are able to sustain a sound after a single beater stroke serves as an introduction to this idea. This can be followed by investigations as to whether the sustained sound is longer or shorter than, for example, five seconds.

Let the children chart environmental sounds, making a recording, so that the sounds can be replayed several times and represented graphically on a sheet of paper. Linear measurement can thus be related to the passage of time. If this exercise is to be turned into an instrumental piece (as described in Chapter 6), the conductor will need to watch a clock in order to make sure that the score is faithfully reproduced.

Chapter 3 describes a timed activity involving sorting a number of tins into similarly sounding pairs. Although the sorting of 'shaky tins' is an activity which ought to be used in the reception year it has, because of the regularly observed failure of children to listen with discrimination, been used in various forms over the whole school age range and, indeed, beyond. Having used the activity in a whole class situation, with individuals taking turns to contribute, one class suggested the idea of sorting against the clock. At first, individuals were timed by a boy who had a stopwatch on his wrist, but the well-known junior desire for complete fairness made it necessary for a proper scrutinised system of timing to be adopted. At this point science and technology were involved in promoting 'a fair test' and when this was established there was a need for a more exciting competition with an undisputed winner.

A pairs competition on a knock-out basis was decided upon, a table designed and playing partners chosen. After a successful run of this competition, the children decided that a better competition would be one in which it was not possible to be knocked out in the first round. Now a league table had to be devised and block diagrams were used to show best performances. Lengths of time had to be very accurately shown on this graph, and the idea that the tallest column always indicated the best achievement was dispelled since in this case the tallest column represented the most time taken. Matches were played at odd times when there was a moment to spare, but rules were drawn up which demanded that these would not count towards the league unless accepted scrutineers were available to validate the procedure.

The selection of scrutineers was most revealing in that some who were high in the pecking order and would be followed in physical activities, were discarded in favour of other children who seemed to be better trusted. An election which was to be held in the school the following day enabled polling booths to be set up and used to ensure secrecy of voting. It was clear that this opportunity resulted in different choices than would have resulted from a show of hands.

The grand final was held between three teams who were equal at the top of the league. Tactics had been developed and were jealously guarded; there was even a suspicion of espionage into the methods employed! Reports had been published daily about the performance of contending teams and, although the class teacher insisted that the whole thing had 'got rather out of hand', he was clearly pleased with the range of activities generated.

Language

Relatively little needs to be said about language since the process of discussion, which must be a constant feature of musical activities, speaks for itself. One hopes that the sterile instruction, 'and when you have finished writing, you can draw a picture' and which was always merely a time filler, is seen for what it is. However, if a child has been carefully

in fact, often dismissed by them as 'silly'. One teacher chose to use the poem, 'The Lady of Shalott' by Alfred Lord Tennyson, with an inner city Y6 class. The descriptions of rivers and towers and knightly virtue could have been dismissed as outside their experience, but the poem was sensitively read and interestingly discussed, and translated into music which was then played while the class mimed. The result was that the poem became a favourite, while music was improvised at each reading. The fact that there were a few cases of near-illiteracy in the class and that English was, for many, a second language did not prevent them from expressing, in music and mime, their feelings and clear understanding of the meaning and mood of the poem.

Science

The methods by which sounds are produced, sustained and transmitted to the ear of the listener have much to do with the shape and appearance of musical instruments. The explanations often sound more scientific than musical. The value of a violin's resonator can be demonstrated by covering the hole in a chime bar with sticky tape and then attempting to make it sound. The column of air inside the resonator, which is carefully made so that it will respond to the vibrations of the associated note, is no longer activated and a dull 'clank' is the result.

This effect can also be demonstrated by passing a piece of card, about one and a half centimetres wide, to and fro over the tone hole of a chime bar just after it has been struck. The result is a 'wobbling' note like the sound made when the hand is repeatedly placed on and removed from the mouth while singing a note; sealing the tone hole on a guitar produces much the same effect.

What, though, causes the air to move? Vibrations can be explored on the sound table with elastic bands stretched round a shoe box. The bands can be seen to vibrate

engaged upon a piece of writing, then transmission of his interest can logically be extended into other fields of expression. This is not to say that the writing necessarily comes first. The stimulus may have come from a visit or a walk and the possibility of music-making may have been discussed at the time. The very process of creating music, or singing about and miming going through a canal tunnel, may act as a magnifying glass through which the details of the visit are later observed and the desire to write about it provoked.

There is much debate about what poetry is suitable for children. For example, many teachers have affirmed that children seemed to enjoy the 'sound' of the poetry of Dylan Thomas while clearly having little idea of what it was about. At the same time there are collections of poems which are intended to make children laugh which are,

when plucked and, as the vibration becomes less wide, so the sound dies away. This is better demonstrated using the lowest string of a guitar. Alternatively, the invisible, high vibrations of a tuning fork can be detected by dipping a ringing tuning fork into water. The vibration of a large cymbal can be demonstrated by dropping grains of rice on to its surface when it is ringing.

The terms 'high' and 'low' in relation to pitch can be explained as having to do with the speed of the vibration, which is why a tightened string makes a higher sound than one under less tension.

Strings of the same length and tension produce the same note, but sounds made with pipes or tubes depend solely upon length. A 'swanee whistle' alters its note when the plunger at the end is pushed in and pulled out in the same way that the trombone works. This instrument demonstrates the principle very well but is, for obvious reasons, better kept in the teacher's desk than on the sound table. Plastic bottles, of equal size, which contain different quantities of water can be blown across to produce different notes.

It has been established that sound is produced by vibrations and that the faster the vibrations move, the higher the note sounds. It was also noted that the deeper the waves of vibration are, the louder the note sounds (Figure 5). It must be pointed out, however, that the sound waves must travel through some medium. This can be demonstrated in the classroom.

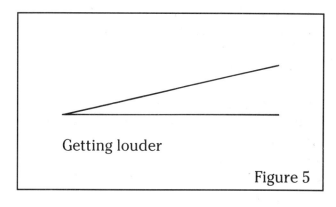

Getting louder

Figure 5

A local secondary school may assist in providing a piece of equipment which shows that without a medium through which sound can travel, sound cannot reach the listener. Place an electric bell in a bell jar, from which air has been pumped with a suction pump. The bell will be audible until the air is pumped out, at which point it will be seen to be ringing but the sound will be either reduced or inaudible.

Demonstrate that sound takes time to travel a distance by asking the children to stand about 100 metres away and then hitting a piece of wood with a hammer. The children will see the wood struck before they hear the sound of the blow.

Sound waves reach the listener at the speed at which they are generated, providing that the listener and the sound source are both still. If a car, sounding its horn, is driven towards listeners, the sound waves arrive faster than the speed at which they are generated because the speed of the car is added to the speed of the waves. As the car passes, the speed of the car is now subtracted from the speed of the sound wave and they arrive at the listener's ear at a *slower* speed at which they are generated. Thus the car's horn appears to sound at a lower pitch as the car passes and disappears into the distance. This is known as 'the Doppler effect'.

The passage of sound waves though a length of wood can be detected by tapping one end, while a child puts her ear to the other end. This was how the principle of the stethoscope was discovered.

Connections between science and music may come when children ask awkward questions at unexpected moments. The science co-ordinator is likely to have planned the examination of matters relating to the generation and transmission of sound, but a knowledge of how musical instruments work and how we hear them will also affect decisions about performance and perhaps even composition.

Chapter 14
Assessment

'The assessment process itself should determine what is to be taught and learned. It should be the servant, not the master, of the curriculum. Yet it should not simply be a bolt-on addition at the end. Rather, it should be an integral part of the educational process, continually providing "feed-back" and "feed-forward"' [Task Group on Assessment and Testing Report, DES, 1988].

In assessing a child's progress in music, the process of 'testing' will play no part, though if one looks at the processes of assessment in music education in the past, the picture was very different. Formal examinations seemed to be the exclusive method of assessment, and a series of fences had to be jumped in order to proceed. It has long been argued that the possession of a pass at Grade 8 is relatively meaningless in terms of assessment of real musicianship, just as the ability of a child to 'get sums right' has been seen as no real indication of mathematical talent. Once it was decided that the ability to write out the melodic minor scale of F# had no connection with the attainment of true 'musicianship' (though, oddly enough, that is what the written paper was called), the process of evaluation became a great deal more complicated. Before, an examiner could award three marks for a correct answer and would knock off a mark for each mistake; now the question is, 'Has this child some spark of musicianship?'

interest and 'D' to the one who gets 'D' for everything else. In order to observe real attainment, it is necessary to make sure that children work in ways in which they are able to reveal their abilities. The constant use of the same groupings will only ensure that a pecking order is established and that the same child always gets the triangle and instructions on what to do with it. Matters of cultural background and gender undoubtedly come into this equation, and the teacher should always seek to reorganise groups and working partners when she sees that some children are getting 'the lamb's share' of responsibility. In this way, it will be easier to assess the child who tries to avoid trouble by adopting a passive role in the same way that he does in the playground, hiding in obscurity and offending no one by advancing ideas which might be rejected because of who he is.

Given that an encouraging working situation can be arranged, one can then begin to form judgements upon more specific matters. Does the child seem to like music? Does she take part in activities and contribute to the work of the group? Is she, when freed of self-doubt or comparison with others, able to exhibit appropriate physical skills? Does she sing in tune when in a large group and can she do so when in a more exposed situation? Does she listen and respond accurately and is she prepared to improvise and to compose? What she has learned is likely to be expressed in what she does and what she says. If she is formally asked to give some sort of right answer or to write it down, the very situation may well produce a 'nil-return', while observation of her activity can reveal a very different picture. A note-book with a page for each child in the class can be very helpful. While observing group activities, the odd meaningful comment can be added to a child's record and, after some time, a useful profile will emerge. This, when considered together with the primary progress charts suggested in Figures 1 and 2, can be found to be of great value.

and 'How is it to be quantified?' Thus, if a teacher is to give credit for a child's progress, or to record that none has been made, she will have to look at considerations other than marks out of ten which reflect the ability to remember the note names of the treble clef. She will also have to balance her judgement in relation to the child's circumstances to avoid the situation of awarding 'A' to the child whose family has a second car which enables her to be taken to private music lessons, 'B' to the child whose parents give encouragement, 'C' to the child who, despite parental indifference, shows some

Key Stage One

Name of child:				
Remarks	Performance Vocal	Played	Composing	Listening and Appraising
	Can copy simple melodic phrases.	Can copy simple rhythmic phrases.	Can take part in simple vocal and instrumental improvisation.	Can recognise musical elements, high, quick, etc.
	Can sing simple songs in tune with control of breath and dynamics.	Can control a range of C/R inst. in simple handling and playing.	Can choose suitable sound sources for specific purposes.	Can identify sounds made by objects and living things.
	Can sing songs with accompaniment of C/R instruments.	Can play simple accompaniments from cues or by rote.	Can improvise simple accompaniments to songs or rhythmic rhymes.	Can discriminate between and discuss qualities of different sounds.
	Can practise and rehearse, responding to direction.		Can justify choice of instruments and playing methods in simple composition.	Can discuss qualities in music and standard of own and others' play.
	Can respond to simple signs and symbols.		Can use simple signs and symbols to record compositions.	Can discuss devices in music and simple musical ideas.
	Able to contribute to and take part in an effective performance.		Can communicate simple musical ideas.	Able to listen attentively to a performance, live or recorded.

Figure 1

Key Stage Two

Remarks	Performance Vocal	Performance Played	Composing	Listening and Appraising
	Can copy and learn by rote songs of moderate complexity.	Can play accompaniments from memory and from simple notations.	Can develop ideas through improvising, composing and arranging.	Understands melody, chords, accompaniment pace and dynamics.
	Sings (unison and 2 part) with understanding of pitch, duration, diction, dynamics and phrasing.	Plays pieces with good dexterity and control. Can hold solo line.	Using widening range of sounds creates music using appropriate musical structures.	Can recognise a range of instruments used in a variety of styles and cultures; shows awareness of mood.
	Can sing a solo part in a group piece.	Can play a solo part in a group piece.	Can choose specific techniques, songs and combinations of sound to create a complete musical shape.	Can recognise general characteristics of music from a number of historical times.
	Can rehearse and direct to develop skills and improve techniques.		Can create music from a range of stimuli using appropriate musical structures.	Can listen and respond to a range of music of different historical and social backgrounds.
	Can take part in an effective performance.		Can record musical ideas through notations which define timbre, dynamics, duration and, where appropriate, pitch.	Can identify music from different styles and genres including opera, folk, jazz and different cultures and traditions.

Figure 2

Observational notes in the 'remarks' column can be used to clarify ticks or marks on the printed boxes. The aspects of work contained in the boxes are only suggested interpretations of the National Curriculum document, and teachers may prefer to develop content of their own. The two charts are intended to cover Key Stages 1 and 2 and a single sheet of this kind could accompany the child throughout the primary years. The division between KS1 and KS2 is somewhat arbitrary since it is clear that, as is seen in all subject volumes of the National Curriculum document, there will be considerable overlap on either side of this line, not only from school to school, but also from child to child.

The order in which the various topic attainments appear on the suggested chart is not some kind of chronological progression; a child's record might appear as in Figure 3.

Key Stage One				
Name of child: *James Wright*				
Remarks	Performance Vocal	Played	Composing	Listening and Appraising
shows good appraisal in oral answers.	Can copy simple melodic phrases.	Can copy simple rhythmic phrases.	Can take part in simple vocal and instrumental improvisation.	Can recognise musical elements, high, quick, etc.
Needs help – 'growler!'	Can sing simple songs in tune with control of breath and dynamics.	Can control a range of C/R inst. in simple handling and playing.	Can choose suitable sound sources for specific purposes. N	Can identify sounds made by objects and living things. N
	Can sing songs with accompaniment of C/R instruments.	Can play simple accompaniments from cues or by rote.	Can improvise simple accompaniments to songs or rhythmic rhymes. N	Can discriminate between and discuss qualities of different sounds. N
Can discuss but doesn't without prodding.	Can practise and rehearse, responding to direction. | N		Can justify choice of instruments and playing methods in simple composition.	Can discuss qualities in music and standard of own and others' play.
Likes dramatic descriptions of music.	Can respond to simple signs and symbols. N		Can use simple signs and symbols to record compositions.	Can discuss devices in music and simple musical ideas.
	Able to contribute to and take part in an effective performance. |		Can communicate simple musical ideas.	Able to listen attentively to a performance, live or recorded.
				Figure 3

The child's teacher writes, 'He joins in class activities in all areas, although he has been observed to be a little clumsy and sometimes reserved. His writing is large, with square shaped letters of unequal sizes. He has made a start at reading, but much prefers to use the story tapes on the listening table. He expresses himself well orally and is particularly interested in science and the natural world, and he gave a short talk to his class on bonsai trees (his mother's hobby), though fell into confusion when asked where bonsai was first practised and he said he had forgotten.

'He enjoys mathematics when it involves handling things and was very much involved in making a graph of pets owned by the class. Though he understood the principle of sticking a picture in the appropriate column for each animal, he had difficulty in interpreting the finished chart. He is quite well liked, but has one particular friend who is more extrovert and who sometimes gets him into trouble.

'In music activities, his listening and imaginative skills seem to be developing well, though he doesn't volunteer his thoughts readily and his motor skills do not yet allow him to clap or play anything much more complicated than a steady rhythm. This quite often has a somewhat jerky quality, though not exactly out of time. He has greater difficulty with an instrument than when clapping, and greater difficulty still when using parts of his body other than clapping. His greatest difficulty is that of pitching his voice, and he needs much kindly encouragement in this area. There are a number of children, predominantly boys, who seem to share his kinds of difficulties, and I plan to let them organise some little compositions about favourite foods, using sung and played word rhythms, and two chime bars which will restrict the singing pitch to the lower vocal register. This will tie up with the project, 'Ourselves', which includes discussion about why we need food and drink, what we like best and why some foods are beneficial and others are not.'

One important thing about this kind of

evaluation is that it seeks to answer the question of what should be done as the school year progresses. Before the National Curriculum, a bit of massed singing with the whole school for half an hour a week was occasionally observed to be the only musical provision; it was too easy to decide that if a child seemed to have no gift for music, then he probably wouldn't need any more provision. However, the inclusion of music in the curriculum has benefits which reach beyond the confines of music itself, and that evaluation of the kind mentioned above enables this wider effect to take place. This kind of record enables *need* to be identified, but is also flexible enough to allow high-flyers to be accommodated.

It is perfectly possible for a child at Key Stage 1 to be able to sing a solo with confidence, to be able to play from simple standard notation and to be able to compose and evaluate a simple melody set to words. These goals appear centrally in the Key Stage 2 section, but in music one may find that the overlap from one key stage to the other is considerable. Children at Key Stage 2 may, on the other hand, need to cover very simple principles. One can envisage a child newly arrived at a junior school, whose musical experience and abilities are unknown. With the use of the kind of approach outlined above, a picture can be gained of the progress which she has already made, and her needs will then be apparent.

The things that children will eventually know should come from the process of practical music-making. The need for *them* to formulate 'rules' to enable them to develop their music-making, without having to start from scratch each session, will be very different from the needs perceived by music teachers in the past. Those needs were met by learning rules at the outset so that children might seem competent, though often without the understanding which comes only from experience. By adopting an approach which is formative as well as summative, we offer the opportunity for children to take part in the assessment of their own work and to identify the need for, for instance, a better kind of notation to record their thoughts. This kind of approach has been seen to lead children to work which a teacher may have thought inappropriate by reason of its advanced nature.

Specialised knowledge

Difficulties have been encountered in movement lessons when children who attended a Saturday morning dance class were involved in imaginative and creative work. Because they had learned specialised ways of managing their bodies, they had stored away a number of clichés which were served up, thus short-circuiting the thinking process. At first sight these children seemed to be the 'best in the class' but, in fact, there were others whose process of creative thought, though they were less physically experienced, was second to none. The question is whether the movements selected come from thoughtful and imaginative intention, or whether they are partial solutions taken 'off the peg'. Don't let the skilled recorder player 'specialise' in creative work. She will be happy to use her skill, and the outcome, as far as the general quality of sound is concerned, will be good. But is she 'hiding' as effectively as the little boy who failed to contribute because he was low in the pecking order?

It is possible that Everton, the large and noisy boy, will make a dive for the large and noisy drum and that Emma, 'who is so sensitive', will always get the full-size glockenspiel. In this situation it will be impossible to see how either are developing. Of course Emma will play the drum accurately and with sensitivity, but is there, lurking beneath Everton's rugged exterior, a quality which has, up to this point, not found means of expression? The opportunity for self-expression within inventive music-making may not exist in so great a measure in any other subject area.

Chapter 15
Using guitar chords

In hundreds of song books one finds, written over the music line, letters and numbers, such as G D7 C, which enable guitar players to accompany the songs.

It is possible to use the guitar chords in any key with classroom instruments. The purpose of this chapter is to explain how this may be done.

Family groups

It is not necessary to know that every key has relatives (relative chords), but it is on this system that Western music is based. For example, the key of C, whose scale starts on the note C, has a 'home' chord called the chord of C, and two near relations, the chords of G and F. There are other relatives but they need not concern us at the moment. In the early days of rock and roll and skiffle, these three most nearly

related chords made vast fortunes for players who 'got by' using only them.

In the key of G, the relative chords are G, C, and D7 (D major seventh), and in the key of D they are D, G and A7. At this stage it is not necessary to know what D major seventh means; the chart on photocopiable page 114 provides the notes making up the chord.

If you hear a piece of music which ends on a chord other than that of the key in which the piece is written, for example, D7 in the key of G, there is a feeling that the piece is not properly ended; because of our cultural musical experience we expect that piece to end on a chord of G.

This key chord may be thought of as 'the home chord' because it gives the feeling of coming home. If one thinks through the National Anthem, but pauses on the last syllable of 'happy and glorious', one is left with the desire to go on until the 'home'

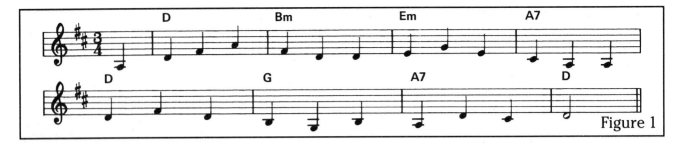

Figure 1

chord is reached. This is, as it happens, the chord of G, while the unsatisfactory stop took place on the chord of D7.

All the chords related to the home chord have parallels in other keys which bear the same relationship to their home chord. Every home chord in every key has, if you like, an 'auntie' chord which is specific to that key as 'auntie' but can also act as the home chord in its own family. For example, the chord of F in the key of C is an 'auntie' chord to the home chord of C. In the key of F, however, F is the home chord while B♭ is the corresponding 'auntie' chord.

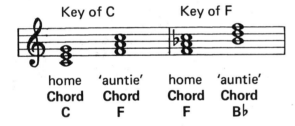

Key of C		Key of F	
home	'auntie'	home	'auntie'
Chord	**Chord**	**Chord**	**Chord**
C	**F**	**F**	**B♭**

As you use the chart on photocopiable page 114 to provide children with notes, you may notice the relationships but no special knowledge is required to do so.

The names of the notes are imprinted on the bars of the glockenspiel, xylophone and chime bars, so when notes are mentioned, they will be easily recognisable.

Figure 1 shows the beginning of a song with guitar chords added at the beginning of every bar. When a small 'm' is written after a letter name of a chord, it means that the chord is a minor chord and has a sadder kind of sound. D means D major chord and is a bright sound; Dm means D minor. By referring to the chart on photocopiable page 114, you can see that the notes for D chord are D, F# and A, while the notes for Dm chord are D, F and A.

The difference in sound can be tried out

on an instrument, but again there is no need to know the difference. Merely looking up the chord's notes on the chart will provide what is required as an accompaniment.

The chords for 'The ash grove' can be played by three children playing simultaneously as follows:

Player 1: A F# B C# A D C# A (5 notes)
Player 2: F# D G A F# B A F# (5 notes)
Player 3: D B E G D G G D (4 notes)

This solution to playing the chords will work, but there are refinements which will make it sound better, and easier to play.

Using fewer notes

Suppose the class were using chime bars. It would be better if one child were to play all the D's while another played all the E's. This would reduce the number of chime bars used and would be very useful if there were not enough bars for duplication of several notes.

If the children were to use glockenspiels, then longish jumps could be avoided. Moreover, if only one child were to use the glockenspiel, the confusion of leaning across another player could be avoided.

For each player to have notes as nearly as possible side by side would produce a smoother effect, so the following adjustment is suggested:

A F# B C# A D C# A
F# D G A F# B A F#
D B E G D G G D

This would produce the following re-arrangement of the chords of 'The ash grove':

108

Player 1: A B B A A B A A (2 notes)
Player 2: F# F# G G F# G G F# (4 notes)
Player 3: D D E C# D D C# D (2 notes)

This is not a matter of music but of logic and can be written out on a grid. As there are fewer notes for each player, the playing procedure is much simpler and well within the ability of the least able.

Repeated sections in songs

Often sections of songs contain repeated music and the 'The ash grove', shown in Figure 1, is no exception. There are four sections to the song but the chord sequence above accompanies the first, the second and the fourth quarters. Only the third part requires different harmonies so it is as well to look at the whole of any song to be arranged so that any repeated parts can be merely marked as repeated and not laboriously written out in full.

What if no chord is indicated?

Sometimes the printer of a song puts in a guitar chord and then there is no indication of a chord for a few bars, as in Figure 2.

This does not mean that the guitar ceases to play, but merely that the chord is to be repeated in subsequent bars until a new chord is written. When arranging such a song it is best to pencil in the repeated chords so that the shape of the harmony is clear.

It will have been noticed that the first of the chords in the tunes shown in Figures 1 and 2 do not happen on the first note. This

is because both tunes start with what is called 'an upbeat' (also known as an anacrucis – an incomplete bar) which is not a strongly emphasised syllable in the words.

The British National Anthem begins very strongly, '*God* save our *Gracious* Queen', and the first chord comes on the strong first beat with no upbeat. The United States National Anthem, on the other hand, has an upbeat, since it starts on a less important word: 'O, *say* can you *see*, in the *dawn's* early *light...*'

Figure 2

109

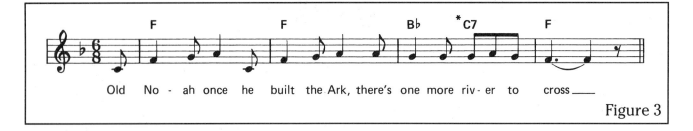

Old No-ah once he built the Ark, there's one more riv-er to cross_____

Figure 3

Chord introductions

The last four chords of the whole song usually make a suitable introduction before the singers start and this gives the whole performance a crisp beginning since the singers receive clues as to the speed of the song, the pitch at which it is to be sung and the exact moment when they are supposed to begin.

Chord changes within a bar

Some songs change a chord in the middle of a bar as in the fourth bar of the example in Figure 3. This means that the players would have to put in a sudden, quicker beat if they had been previously playing only on the first beat of the bar. For this reason, it is best that the chords written in bars on their own be played twice in each bar and be written out as in Figure 4. Thus if a change of chord occurs halfway through the bar, it will merely involve a change of note and not a change of rhythm.

Chords	F		F	
Words Old No-ah once he built the Ark,				
Played	*	*	*	*
Chords	Bb	C7	F	
Words there's one more ri-ver to cross				
Played	*	*	* *	

Figure 4

The grid which the children would play would look like Figure 5.

F	F	F	F	Bb	C7	F	F
C	C	C	C	D	C	C	C
A	A	A	A	Bb	Bb	A	A
F	F	F	F	F	E	F	F

Figure 5

After a little practice at transcribing simple songs from guitar chords and using them in class, you will see how useful this technique can be. This, however, is only one of the uses of chord grids.

Using chord families for composition

Once the children are familiar with their use, they can go on to organise chords for themselves using the chord family cards (see Chapter 20, page 165). These cards provide a scale from which a melody can be composed and the chords which can be used to make accompaniments. Once a composition has been made, it can be played on classroom instruments or with the use of electronic keyboards. Alternatively, a composition made on keyboards can be transcribed for use by a classroom orchestra.

It is difficult to say at what age children can handle various activities because levels of attainment and experience differ so much from one situation to another. The organisation of chords into a harmonic sequence could well begin in Y5, but it is likely that, with the right previous experience, this activity could be successful a year earlier. Playing the accompaniment of a song in this manner has certainly been successfully undertaken in a top infant class.

Once all children in the class have taken turns at playing from a grid in both class and group situations, you can begin to try the progression which leads to the organisation of chords and more advanced uses of the electronic keyboard.

Beginning to compose

After playing from prepared grids related to songs, the next step is to provide a grid of chords over which a melody can be composed, as in Figure 6.

Give a group of children the grid, plus the chime bars necessary for playing the chords, a couple of unpitched instruments and a glockenspiel. Then ask them to play the chord sequence, adding melody and rhythmic accompaniment. They may

choose to make a cumulative piece in which a drum starts followed at intervals by a tambourine and the chime bars and finally the tune. The tune can last for a number of repetitions of the chords. At first these tunes will tend to ramble on with very little shape. With experience, however, more recognisable tune lengths will develop. This can be encouraged by providing a simple four line rhythm to be made into a song. This kind of activity works very well within a rolling group work programme when children take turns at participating in science, maths, art, language and music activities.

The obvious extension of this activity is for the children to be able to organise the

CHORD FAMILY OF C – the notes of the scale are:

C, D, E, F, G, A, B, C.

G	G	A	A	G	G	G	G
E	E	F	F	F	F	E	E
C	C	C	C	B	B	C	C
Chord C		Chord F		Chord G7		Chord C	

Figure 6

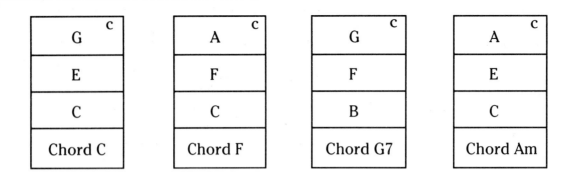

	c		c		c		c
G		A		G		A	
E		F		F		E	
C		C		B		C	
Chord C		Chord F		Chord G7		Chord Am	

The small letter at each top right-hand corner of the cards indicates the chord family to which the card belongs so that sets can be made up after use.

Figure 7

chords either to fit an existing tune or for composition of their own melody. This can be done when they have had plenty of practice in using chord family cards and have begun to be accustomed to the sounds produced by them. Sets of cards can be made as in Figure 7, rather like chord family cards cut into separate pieces. You will notice that there is an extra card in this set, namely A minor. This appears on the grid of families of chords on page 114, but can be omitted if only C, G7 and F have been used in the composition activity. There are two more members of the family; these can be found in the chord family and scales section of Chapter 20.

Let the children make their own grid and fill in the chosen chords in the same way as was earlier shown for the song 'Old Noah'

(see page 110). Work cards similar to that in Figure 8 can be kept with the chord cards.

A final activity in this area would be to let children find an accompaniment to a known song. This does not mean that they have to find 'the' accompaniment, which the composer or arranger chose.

The work card in Figure 9 opposite contains the six chords of the immediate family for the key of G. The individual chord cards which were moved around during the making of the accompaniment can be envisaged.

If you have never considered this kind of work before, don't feel too daunted if you cannot take it all in immediately. Start by just trying out some of the initial activities with the children, adding to the

Work Card 5 – COMPOSING WITH CHORD CARDS
You can choose to compose in the key of C, or G, or F.
The scale of C is – C, D, E, F, G, A, B and C.
　　　　　　G is – G, A, B, C, D, E, F# and G.
　　　　　　F is – F, G, A, B♭, C, D, E and F.
Write a tune and accompaniment for these words:
The moonlight's on the water, the wind is blowing free;
The harbour lights, they twinkle as the ships go out to sea.

Figure 8

D	E	D	E	E	D
B	C	C	C	B	B
G	G	F#	A	G	F#
G	C	D7	Am	Em	Bm

Try out these chords to make an accompaniment for a song you know.

Scale of G: G, A, B, C, D, E, F#, G.

Make sure you can sing it in this key.

Figure 9

complexities as and when they are ready to progress. In fact, the use of guitar chords is straightforward and has been welcomed by non-specialist students and teachers alike. Children seem to have the least problem of all.

Chord families, page 107

C	*	C	E	G
F		F	A	C
G7		F	G	B
Am		A	C	E
D	*	D	F#	A
G		G	B	D
A7		G	A	C#
Bm		B	D	F#
E♭	*	E♭	G	B♭
A♭		A♭	C	E♭
B♭7		A♭	B♭	D
Cm		C	E♭	G
E	*	E	G#	B
A		A	C#	E
B7		A	B	D#
G#m		G#	B	D#

F	*	F	A	C
B♭		B♭	D	E♭
C7		B♭	C	E
Dm		D	F	A
G	*	G	B	D
C		C	E	G
D7		C	D	F#
Em		E	G	B
A	*	A	C#	E
D		D	F#	A
E7		D	E	G#
F#m		F#	A	C#
B♭	*	B♭	D	F
E♭		E♭	G	B♭
F7		E♭	F	A
Gm		G	B♭	D

1) Write down required chords.
2) Write down notes.
3) Re-arrange notes as described in text.
4) Asterix (*) indicates 'home' chord.

Chapter 16
Electronic equipment

There are a number of basic kinds of instruments and machines which may be of use in the primary classroom, but each one appears on the market in a bewildering array of shapes and forms. The cost can range from about ten pounds to many hundreds of pounds, and practically none of it can solve, on its own, a teaching need, despite much glossy advertising. The teacher needs to have a certain amount of commitment to, and knowledge of, this area, and to attend in-service courses if she intends to include these remarkable resources in an exciting and fruitful teaching programme.

Tape recorders

The tape recorder is the most familiar piece of electronic equipment. These range from the 'throw away' variety which are not intended to be repaired when they become defective, to highly expensive machines with twin cassettes and the facility to add sounds to an already recorded track known as a 'dubbing facility'. A useful machine which costs little is the old-fashioned reel-to-reel tape recorder which, if it has three speeds, can provide an interesting resource for experimental composition.

Of all the services able to be rendered by a tape recorder, that of making a good recording of children's work and playing it back in good quality sound is the most important. For this purpose a solid cassette recorder of good quality is desirable. It should be able to be operated by the children without involving the use of a perplexing number of controls. An internal microphone is useful, although these sometimes tend to provide less good sound quality than the sort that plug in and stand apart from the machine. This, however, is somewhat more vulnerable in the class situation and its use must be carefully managed. The uses of this, and second-hand reel-to-reel machines, will be described later in the chapter.

Sound processing units

These machines are most likely to be appropriate in Y5, Y6 and Y7, and then only when there is a member of staff who has, at least, attended an in-service course on the subject. Remarkable effects which include echoing, delaying and altering the speed of sounds and playing them backwards can be achieved. However, it must be stressed that these items are not toys: if children are to use them in creative work, they need to know what the equipment is capable of and work towards what they intend and not merely string together a series of accidents. They cannot, therefore, merely be introduced, but their use must be built up to in a carefully planned programme by someone who understands their use and value.

Drum machines

Drum machines not only produce sounds which are similar to the set rhythms included in the variety of effects which are built into keyboards, but also have pads which are struck with drumsticks and produce a variety of drum sounds. In the more expensive types, it is also possible to play pitched percussion notes. It is possible to set them to play a drum rhythm which can then be added to by the player. There is little point in using a drum machine with children who have not already played real drums, just as drums cannot be played successfully until facility has been gained in clapping and tapping rhythms.

Multi-track tape recorders

Multi-track tape recorders are often described as 'portable mini studios' since separate instruments can be recorded one after the other and the tracks played back together. Often a separate amplifier and loud-speaker are required if performances are to be heard other than on headphones. The multi-track tape recorder is a valuable, but expensive, item which, realistically, could be fully exploited only by a teacher who is knowledgeable and enthusiastic about music information technology. With this knowledge, which is much easier to gain than many suppose, children in the later primary years can become involved in highly stimulating activities which will stretch their listening and problem solving abilities to the limit.

The problems of availability of the equipment are, of course, similar to those experienced by classes with a single computer. There is, moreover, an additional problem of providing silent recording conditions when using a microphone.

Midi equipment

Midi stands for Musical Instrument Digital Interface. An 'interface' is really like an interpreter at a conference. It receives information in the form given out by an instrument and translates it into the form understood by a computer. The computer can then transform the information according to the program being used, and cause the midi equipment to play it back in an altered form. Keyboard, guitar and horn effects can be produced.

Some computers are able to print out music which has been entered from a 'midi' instrument, which fulfils the musician's long-held dream of a music typewriter.

Theoretically these instruments could be used in primary schools, though there are many practical reasons, cost and teaching

resources among them, which suggest that they are more likely to be found in secondary schools. Midi microphones capable of receiving the sounds of acoustic instruments for computer treatment are in the process of being developed but are, at the time of writing, not completely satisfactory. Advances are being made all the time, and any teachers interested should contact their local advisory centre to discover what stage of development has been reached.

Keyboards

This is an area in which the choice is simply bewildering. Each model has its own set of facilities which needs to be understood if the instrument is to be used to advantage. Among obvious differences, the actual keys are made in a variety of sizes which can be anything from full piano size to those so small as to make playing by an adult virtually impossible.

Small keys

A pianist or organist might have reservations about machines with very small keys as the transition to full size keys might pose difficulties. However, in the experimental stages of electronic keyboard use this need not be a difficulty. The keyboard, after all, is merely a sound source. Children who are working towards Key Stage One and are engaged in discovering the characteristics of sounds available, will 'poke' at the instrument with single fingers and thus find out the relationship of hand position to high and low notes, that volume is controllable and that different sound qualities are available from the set of 'stops'. They will also discover that if the machine is not switched on, it will not work. Once the basics are understood, the instrument can be used as a classroom sound source in the same way as one would use a glockenspiel or a drum.

What is a sampler?

There are small and inexpensive keyboards which provide a facility called a 'sampler'. This enables a child to speak a word (for instance, 'Hello'), which will then be played back as though being sung at the pitch on any note played. If you sing the National Anthem with 'hello' as the word for each note, you will see how the effect sounds. Any sound can be put into the memory and its quality will be reproduced, but at the appropriate pitch, as each note is played. Having discovered that a tune can be made more interesting with the use of the sampler, some method of playing which is more agile than the two-finger method will be needed.

Building up finger technique

Larger, near standard-size keys become valuable when children begin to need to play phrases of music which require the use of individual fingers. This does not come naturally to many children but the improvisation of tunes on five notes – C, D, E, F and G – can help individual use of the fingers and may lead to an invented notation involving numbers.

Play-back facility

Many keyboards have a play-back facility. This enables a phrase which has just been played to be repeated. The children may find this initially interesting, but it has little value in the early stages of keyboard playing. It is better for a child who wishes to record and repeat a phrase to do so physically using a tape recorder, as this familiarises the child with the recording process and enables a number of attempts to be made so that the best attempt can be chosen.

Touch sensitivity

Some instruments are 'touch sensitive'. This means that they respond to finger pressure as should a piano. This kind of instrument is much more expensive than the ordinary 'organ touch' type, and in order to justify the expense, firm ground work should be undertaken by the children. A salesperson may give a number of reasons why the touch sensitive model is preferable but, while a valuable refinement, this facility is not a necessity.

Polyphonic keyboards

In the early days of keyboard sales, small instruments could be bought which were 'monophonic'. This means that they could play only one note at a time. These are still available, but have no real practical use in school because the experience which they are able to provide can also be had from a 'polyphonic' instrument. These are so called because they can play many notes at the same time. The number of notes concurrently available varies from model to model but none is so limited as to make it unable to be of use in the average primary school.

Durability

No firm which sells keyboards is likely to describe a product as a 'school model', as this might give the impression of something rather basic. This is unfortunate, as teachers like to know which model can take a bit of rough handling and survive the insensitive proddings which characterise a child's first attempts at playing. Dealers can provide information of this sort, if asked, though such durability is not usually their first consideration. Do not be afraid to ask, because many schools have suffered disappointments when an otherwise excellent piece of equipment has proved unsuitable on this score. If it cannot be operated by children, then it is a waste of money.

Simplicity

This leads to a further consideration which has been touched on earlier in this chapter. The equipment must be simple enough for primary children to use. There must be no complications which will cause a child to 'opt out' and be unwilling to risk experimentation in case he seems to have failed to make the equipment work. Some might grasp the workings of the instrument, but others might not which could result in failure to take advantage of an exciting resource.

Synthesisers

Synthesisers are very varied, complicated and expensive pieces of equipment and should not be confused with keyboards. Considerable skill is required to use them effectively: unless they are under the control of someone thoroughly conversant with their use, they will contribute little to school music. To try to describe what may be achieved would take a whole book, or an in-service course of considerable length; anyone interested should seek direct assistance from a local teachers' centre where a synthesiser can be used and

explained. The important thing is to realise that when a keyboard is needed, a synthesiser should not be purchased. It is a very specialised piece of equipment which can, nevertheless, be used effectively in primary schools. It is, however, not something which a primary teacher should naturally see as a priority purchase.

Electricity

Before using any piece of equipment which relies upon electrical current, there is something which must be made absolutely clear to children. They may have used bulbs, motors, buzzers and batteries in technology, and they may have handled the bare copper wire which is sometimes used. They know that the little nine-volt batteries are completely harmless and will have used them with confidence. Now they might be handling a cassette recorder which can use either batteries or be plugged into the mains, so there might seem no reason why the power from the wall plug should be any more feared than the batteries, since the tape recorder runs equally well from each power source. It must, therefore, be made clear at the outset that wall-plug power is a killer.

A dummy plug should always reside in the electrical socket when it is not in use, and the switch should also be turned off. A dummy plug can simply be an unused plug with no wire attached to it. When wishing to use a power socket, a routine such as the following should be taught and enforced:
• Check that the dummy plug is in and that the switch is in the 'off' position.
• Make sure the end of the lead which goes into the equipment is securely in and the machine turned off and in the position in which it is to be used.
• Take out the dummy plug and plug in the three-pin plug on the piece of equipment's lead. Make sure that there is no gap between the plug and socket. If you are using an extension lead, check while the power is still off that the connection is also firmly home.
• Switch on the power switch and then switch on the equipment. If nothing happens, switch the mains off and tell your teacher. Never investigate the failure.
• When you have finished with the equipment, switch off the machine, switch off the power point and replace the dummy plug.

Caring for equipment

When equipment is in use, it is best not to allow access for children to walk round it. However, if this is unavoidable, then a piece of carpet should be placed over any trailing wire. There should be a permanent dust-free place in a lockable cupboard for each machine. Never let chalk dust settle on a machine, and occasionally dust it with a soft, dry cloth. If the keys become grubby, wipe them with a cloth, slightly dampened with methylated spirits.

Fuses

If you discover that a fuse in a plug has blown, then make sure that it is replaced by a fuse of the same power. Electronic equipment uses a very small amount of electricity, and if it is over-loaded, severe damage can occur. The fuse is an intentional weak link in the power chain, so that if a greater amount of power begins to flow, the weak link gives way, isolating the valuable electronics. If a fuse which has blown is replaced by one which allows a larger passage of power, then the equipment will not be protected. If a three-amp fuse is replaced by one which allows thirteen amps to flow, for example, then there is a real danger of damage.

The blowing of a fuse is a warning, not that the fuse is too small, but that there is a possible fault. If a second fuse of similar small size burns out, switch off, disconnect the machine and report the fault. A fuse can sometimes blow for no particular reason and simple replacement with a similar fuse is all that is required. It is not always possible to see when a fuse has blown, so by replacing it you can carry out a simple check which may reveal the trouble.

The following checklist may be of use when a tape recorder fails to work.

If the machine fails to play back when using a plug and the power light is off:
• Check the power connection to machine.
• Check that the power socket is switched on.
• Check that the tape recorder is switched on.
• Check that all plugs are fully home.
• Open the plug(s) and check that no wires are loose.
• Change the fuse.   If the power light is on and the reels move but no sound comes out, the volume knob is probably turned right down.

If battery power is being used, and the machine fails to run:
• Check that the power lead from the plug is not plugged in. This will isolate the batteries in many models.

• Check that the batteries are properly inserted and the compartment door is closed.

• Replace the batteries.

If the machine still fails to work, make sure that the 'pause' button hasn't been left in the pressed position before you report the fault.

Introducing keyboards

Let us imagine that a small keyboard costing about twenty pounds has been purchased and is about to be introduced to a class who have never used one.

The difference between battery power and the mains should be explained, though for this purpose we shall assume that the machine is operated by batteries. The on/off switch should be explained and any light which indicates the status of the switch should be noted. The ability to produce different sound qualities should then be explained and the method of controlling the volume pointed out. The principle of pitch (high and low notes) should be introduced or revised and the children should be invited to switch on, adjust the volume and select a sound.

Later, an opportunity should be provided for them to experiment simply. When a composition is listened to, discussion of the instrument's facilities should take place, so that future users will benefit from and add to their knowledge of the instrument's capabilities. It may be that a child will discover an effect that has previously not been heard. This may involve any sort of instrument and not just the keyboard, but this method of thinking and evaluating performances will add to the general knowledge of instrumental possibilities. A poor sound, inappropriate to the mood of the composition, may be identified, or a new 'rule' may be formulated in the minds of the listeners (the future composers) to help them avoid an ugly sound.

The reel-to-reel tape recorder

The tape recorder I was given for my twenty-first birthday still has a use. As big as a suitcase and as heavy as two buckets of water, it occasionally comes out of retirement and delights children who are hardly big enough to lift it. Many old machines have three speeds, the middle speed being the one normally used: this can lead to all sorts of investigation into sound.

The giant's tale

When a voice was recorded and played back at a slower speed, one class of children found that they could make the sound of a giant speaking. However, the giant 'spoke' so slowly that it was difficult to hear what he was saying, so the children realised that the words to be recorded

would have to be spoken very fast in order to come out at normal speaking speed. The children then devised a story with a speaking part for the giant, but when they recorded it they found that there were pauses before the giant spoke because of the gaps in the tape.

The teacher suggested that the whole finished story should then be recorded and this was done using a cassette recorder and a microphone through which the final tape was recorded.

The deep bell of a castle was needed, and the children knew immediately what to do. A chime bar was recorded at high speed, slowed down and recorded on to another tape recorder. This was then replayed at normal speed on the reel-to-reel tape recorder and slowed down a second time to make the pitch even lower.

The unevenness of the bell strokes was very disappointing. Plans had to be made to re-record the bell strokes at exactly even intervals and at high speed, while other children began to work on the creepy music which described the castle before the bell began to ring. This was later recorded on the reel-to-reel machine and the playback was distorted by touching the spool as it unwound.

The final performance before an audience of infant children one playtime was illustrated by pictures on a 'television' made from a cardboard box.

Acquiring new equipment

As the term went on, the children began to identify needs for new equipment. They wanted to be able to add one sound to another without the poor balance and loss of sound quality which resulted from an acoustic recording being made from an acoustic recording of an acoustic recording! A small portable recording studio, such as the primary school version of the Tascam multi-track machine was clearly the answer, and the need for it was identified by the children themselves. A sponsored relay marathon round the school was brightly suggested by a deputation to the headteacher.

This example illustrates how a stock of electronic instruments needs to be built up naturally and according to need. In this way, teachers and children have the chance to learn together about the method of operation and uses of items of equipment; it is depressing when an expensive piece of equipment is hardly ever used. It is for this reason that the school co-ordinator for information technology needs to educate colleagues in the use of such equipment, and not merely appear as a technician when equipment is to be used.

Chapter 17
Ethnic music

The term 'ethnic music' tends to be used to describe music of 'other' cultures, many of which enrich the cultural life of the British Isles. However, the heritage of songs from the British Isles can be shared by those who have become recent residents in the same way as their music has become available to those accustomed to the indigenous English, Scottish, Welsh or Irish traditions.

Sharing music

'Why are you crying?' asked a teacher of a little nine-year-old Asian girl who was suddenly in floods of tears.

'Oh, Sir, it is so beautiful.'
Narjinda was crying for Flora MacDonald who had just waved goodbye to Bonnie Prince Charlie as he escaped to France. 'Will ye no come back again?' had been used in a music lesson and she had shared a moment which had no national boundaries, nor feelings which needed translation from one culture to another.

Sharing is the most important aspect of multicultural understanding, and it is easy to share music. This chapter will attempt to describe ways in which children can make music in styles related to specific cultures. Few can achieve the skill of a real tabla player or handle a kloboto with the skill of an accomplished African drummer. What is possible is that elements of a particular 'ethnic' music can be used in the classroom so that when a recording or performance is heard, the children can identify with the performers and, in some degree, understand what they hear. To

population by these means. The outbreak of war was similarly signalled. (We should remember that the word 'belfry', the place where bells are hung, refers not to the bells but to the Latin word *bellum* which means 'war'.)

Harmony, which is a vital and complicated part of Western music, is much less important in African music, but the use of rhythm in tremendously complicated forms is its basic building block. These exciting rhythms are beginning to appear in Western music, but they are directly borrowed from Africa and have not been developed within Western culture. Like language, music can be enriched by borrowings from other cultures. For example, there were considerable borrowings from English music in about 1400 by continental composers and the outcome was re-borrowed by English composers nearly 200 years later; the product of this exchange was the English madrigal and the blossoming of 'The Golden Age' of English music with composers such as Weelkes, Willbye and Morley.

African musical instruments

Although African music uses a great variety of instruments, the drum and the 'gong-gong', which is rather like a two-tone cow bell, are the most usual basic sounds around which musical structures are built. The experience of the kinds of rhythms used can, however, be introduced using clapping and simple classroom instruments. The luxury of real African drums, which can be bought fairly cheaply, can be dispensed with until successful use of the rhythms justifies the expense. Commercial copies of African drums are less satisfactory than the real thing and also tend to be more expensive. Advice about African instruments can be had from AKLOWA (Centre for Traditional African Drumming and Dancing), Takeley House, Brewer's End, Takeley, Near Bishop's

describe 'African' music in a few sentences would be rash, since that huge continent is rich in musics of various and contrasting kinds. Some attempt, however, will be made to suggest ways in which African drum music can be used in the junior classroom so that the wonder of it can be better appreciated. A number of ethnic musics will be considered in this way so that some kind of understanding and sharing will be possible.

African music

There is an interesting parallel between the traditional use of church bells in Britain and the drums of Africa. News of ceremonies, festivals, births, deaths and marriages are, or were in the case of church bells, communicated to the

Stortford, Hertfordshire, and the African Centre, King Street, Covent Garden, London.

African rhythms in the classroom

Before attempting to use recognisably African rhythms, set up a simplified activity into which the more complicated rhythms can later be introduced. Start by using a rhythm grid, as in Figure 1, to provide a notation from which the children can play and, later, record their own rhythmic compositions. The asterisks mark the beats and the beginning of each line is stressed.

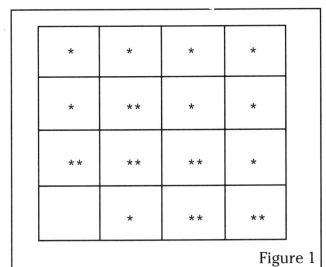

Figure 1

Start by clapping single lines, then the whole grid, line by line. Alternatively, one half of the class can clap one line while a second group claps another. The grid can also be played as a round, the second group joining in from the beginning when the first has reached the second line. Similarly, four groups can play a repeated line each, or follow each other as a four-part round. The rhythms contained in the grid can be provided by the teacher or invented by the children themselves so that use of rhythm grids not only increases facility in 'sight reading' but also builds up rhythmic and physical skills and suggests a method by which composed rhythms can be recorded.

Words from a well-known round can be used to produce a surprisingly African-sounding combination of rhythms:
Row, row, row your boat
Gently down the stream,
Merrily, merrily, merrily, merrily,
Life is but a dream.
A way in which words from this round can be used is shown in Figure 2. The rhythm can be spoken, clapped and spoken and, finally, just clapped. When the three lines can be played together, using instruments, an excellent 'African' effect is achieved.

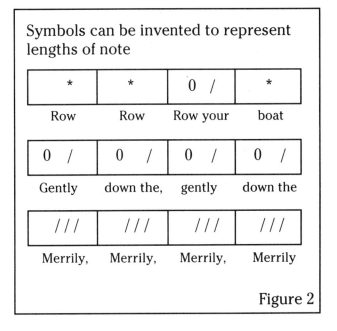

Figure 2

Figure 3 shows an exercise which can be played using a rhythm grid. It involves what are known as 'cross rhythms'. These are so called because the stress does not fall where the European ear expects them, but 'cross' the tidy, equal-length phrases

This example 'seems' to have seven beats in the bar which makes it more tricky.

Figure 3

upon which the Western tradition is based. The stress (indicated by the underlined symbol) does not fall at the beginning of the bar because there are no bars. Line three will prove particularly difficult and this, as all lines, should be carefully practised until the players are fully familiar with the rhythm and can play without referring to the grid. Each group should play only their single repeated line.

Children seem to have less difficulty with cross rhythms than adults who have become, in some measure, music specialists. A similar phenomenon was seen with a group of recorder players who had some medieval music to play which was written before bar lines were invented. While the teacher counted furiously, the children seemed to deal with the difficult rhythms far more naturally, unencumbered, it seemed, by too much education.

After the work of putting it together has been done, introduce the use of instruments of different sounds for each line to allow the textures resulting from the cross rhythms to be heard more clearly. The first line could be played on bongos so that the stressed beat is played on the larger drum and the other on the smaller one. In the same way, line two could be played on a two-tone cowbell and the third line on a two-tone block. Similar compositions can be put together by children in groups and tried out at the end of a lesson.

Dancing

Although music of this kind can be rehearsed in a whole-class situation, it is clearly not possible for all the class to play at once. This, however, is an excellent opportunity to encourage the children to dance to their own music. A number of African music groups who provide workshops in schools and colleges include this kind of activity in their programmes. A basic approach might be to ask the players to begin their music and encourage the dancers to begin to move as the music seems to suggest. If possible, arrange a demonstration by someone who has seen or done such dancing. This will prove infectious, and soon the whole group will be taking part. At a pre-arranged signal, everyone should stop dancing while one chosen person dances on her own. Encourage those watching to clap improvised rhythms and cheer on the soloist. After a short time, let everyone join in again until someone else is chosen.

Polyrhythmic music

Polyrhythms are discussed in Chapter 11 in another form but, in the context of African drumming, individual rhythmic phrases of different lengths played at the same time will produce ever-changing cross rhythms. Figure 4 illustrates a piece for three instruments. In this example one player starts and the second can begin at any time later, followed by the third player. Because the rhythms are of different lengths, they continuously produce different patterns which are varied and often interesting.

The above-mentioned approaches give a flavour of African music-making, but can do little more than whet the appetite. Some ideas for further exploration of this area of music are given in Chapter 20.

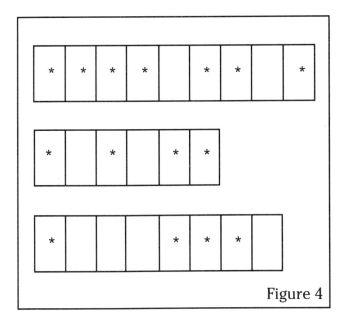

Figure 4

Caribbean music

The history of the development of calypso singing is closely linked with the social history of the West Indies and any project work done in that area would be

incomplete without attempting this attractive kind of music-making. The histories of calypso and reggae tell much about Caribbean culture. In a project about the Caribbean it will not be enough to sing 'Jamaica farewell' with piano accompaniment.

Calypso

Calypso singing is traditionally concerned with the use of words which are improvised to fit a particular occasion. The West Indies' cricket tour of England in the 1950s produced 'Cricket, lovely cricket' which celebrated their success. This was, in at least one way, typical in that the calypso was traditionally 'boasting' music. In the 1960s in the famous BBC television programme *That Was The Week That Was*, Lance Percival, a guitar-playing humorist and actor, was given topical subjects about

Calypso rhythm

1	2	3	4	1	2	3	4									
*	x*		*	*	x*		*	*	x*		*	*	x*		*	Wood block
*	**	*	**	*	**			*	**	*	**	*	**			Claves
			*			*				*					*	Struck shaker
**	*	**	*	**	*	**	*	**	*	**	*	**	*	**	*	Tapped tambourine
*		*	*	*		*	*	*		*	*	*		*	*	Small drum
*		*		*		*		*		*		*		*		Big drum

Figure 5

which he would make an instant calypso. Although remarkably clever, the 'calypsos' had little of the real West Indian flavour and only qualified as such because of the element of improvisation. Modern calypso singing has to compete, in terms of polish, with all forms of widely heard popular music, so although conceived as an improvision, there is a good deal of 'improvement' before performance with characteristic rhythms and harmonies.

Figure 5 shows how the basic calypso rhythm may be played in the primary classroom. If the children are accustomed to working from a rhythm grid, let groups make copies of the grid and practise the rhythms using clapping, tapping and so on. If possible, let them listen to some recorded calypso music before attempting this exercise so that they can understand the style of playing and catch the infectious gaiety of the rhythms.

The process of inventing words and tunes and using the chord cards (see Chapters 15 and 20) to fit chordal accompaniments to them may well follow, but the example in Figure 6 can be used to bridge the gap between rhythmic playing and composing. Chords are provided but a tune needs to be composed. Encourage the children to make up some words first. (Words often tend to be about how awful school is, but this is in keeping with the early history of the calypso which was sung in languages that the plantation bosses couldn't understand!)

A possible chord sequence for a calypso

Player																	
1	A	A	A	A	A	A	A	A	C	B	A	A	A	B	A	A	Requires A, B, C.
2	F#	G	G	F#	F#	G	G	F#	F#	G	G	F#	F#	G	G	F#	Requires F# and G.
3	D	C#	C#	D	D	C#	C#	D	D	D	C#	D	D	D	C#	D	Requires C# and D.
	D	A7	A7	D	D	A7	A7	D	D7	G	A7	D	D	G	A7	D	

*	**		*	Play this rhythm on each note.

Add these chords to the rhythms written above, then add a tune and sing it.

Figure 6

Reggae

Reggae is a much more recent development than calypso though it shares the same strong Afro-Caribbean roots. It became associated with the religion of Ras Tafari (Rastafarianism) and became a means by which this religion, well known in Jamaica for many years, was brought to wider notice.

The rhythms are insistent and very much characterised by putting rhythmic emphasis on 'weak beats'. A vocal use of these rhythms can be made. Figure 7 gives an example, in which the class is divided

*	*	*	*	*	*	*	*	Group 1
	*		*		*		*	Group 2
	**		**		**		**	Group 3
		*				*		Group 4
**	**	**	**	**	**	**	**	Group 5

This is a grid of the rhythms for use when working in groups with instruments.

Figure 7

into five groups. In this example, the first group could be asked to tap their knees, while a second group taps the floor, the third and fourth groups speak (for example, 'chakka, chakka' and 'boom, boom') and the fifth group claps lightly. Working in groups, children can put these rhythms together using body sounds or instruments and can practise 'rapping' or speaking rhythmically against the rhythm. You will possibly find that, once the rhythmic framework has been set up, experts reveal themselves. However, unless one or two children have some interest and experience of this kind of vocal work, or a recorded example is available, this kind of work is not likely to prosper, although the rhythms shown above can be used to accompany the many reggae-type songs which are in print.

The chords which are often heard playing the above rhythms are fairly simple. The example in Figure 8 can be repeated over and over again.

Indian music

It would be rash to try to describe the music of any culture in just a few paragraphs. Within the Indian subcontinent there are eight huge regions, each with its distinct folk music culture. Furthermore, the various religious musical traditions reflect complicated interrelationships and inputs which include the influence of Western music. In addition to this kind of music, there is a strong tradition of classical music, which may provide some kind of classroom experience of India's rich musical culture.

Simple reggae chord sequence

	*		*		*		*		*		*		*		*
G	G	G	G	A	A	A	A	B	B	B	B	A	A	A	A
E	E	E	E	F	F	F	F	G	G	G	G	F	F	F	F
C	C	C	C	D	D	D	D	E	E	E	E	D	D	D	D

This can be played one-handed on the piano, moving the fingers up one note each time and then returning in the same way.
An emphasis should be placed on the starred chords.

Figure 8

Elements in Indian classical music

The drone

The drone is a very simple device which involves two or more notes sounding continuously. Built into the variety of bagpipes which are found in many lands, it forms an important element in northern European folk music. In Indian music, it is played by a four-stringed instrument called the tambura. The drone sounds continuously and produces a characteristic foundation over which the melody is played.

Melody

Three instruments can be used to play the melody part. These are the familiar sitar, the smaller sarangi and a small flute without any keys. The melodies played by these instruments are built on *ragas*. There are well over 200 *ragas* in Indian music. These are scale-like groups of notes, each of which evoke a specific mood or feeling. There are *ragas* expressing happiness, sadness, courage, excitement and humour, as well as *ragas* for morning, afternoon and night, to mention but a few.

Rhythm

A pair of drums known as the tabla play the *tala*, a rhythmic sequence that is repeated over and over again. This is always the same length with the same basic beats, but contains variations improvised by the player. There are said to be 360 *talas*. As the music progresses, so the speed increases and more complicated variations are improvised by both melody and rhythm players until a tremendous climax is reached.

Improvisation

Although there are means of remembering and recording the details of *ragas* and rhythms, performed Indian music is not written down. It is therefore difficult to guess how Indian music has changed over the years although, because of its nature, it may have sounded similar for thousands of years. The *ragas* were classified in an important musical commentary in the thirteenth century and detailed descriptions of the *talas* were recorded 2,000 years ago, but the actual practice of performance over the years can only be assumed.

The Indian classical player who improvises must use the prescribed notes of the chosen *raga*. These are sometimes different when going up and coming down. This is not so strange as it may sound, as precisely the same rule applies to the melodic minor scale in the European tradition. In fact, a tune in a minor key would seem very awkward to a Western ear if it did not follow this same kind of rule.

Playing drones

In many instruments, such as the bagpipes or hurdy-gurdy, the drone is a continuous sound, but when played on the tambura, the notes are separate. A sustained effect is obtained because the notes continue to sound when the string is struck as happens when a guitar string is plucked. A similar effect can be obtained on an electronic keyboard with the 'sustain' button switched on, and if it has a 'harpsichord' effect which can be used at the same time, then something akin to the real sound of the tambura can be produced.

Each *raga* has a drone specific to its use, so I shall consider the playing of drones in a section which deals with the sound of specific *ragas*.

Ragas

As has been previously mentioned, *ragas* relate to a specific mood or time of day. The 'night' *raga*, *malakosh*, is peaceful and meditative, and its accompanying drone is shown in Figure 9.

This *raga* is useful for a first attempt at improvisation since the notes ascending and descending are the same. Thus the beginner does not have to think about the progression of notes which would come

naturally to an experienced player. Merely to improvise on these notes without real knowledge would, however, not produce music acceptable to the Indian ear, but simply 'make an Indian sound'. The relationships between notes (rather like the relationships between chords in Western music mentioned in Chapter 15) cannot be simply explained. Suffice it to say that the most important note which is often repeated is called *vadi*, or 'king' note. The *samvadi*, the 'chief minister', is the next important note. There is also the *anuvadi*, the 'servant' note. Lastly there is the *vivadi*, the 'enemy' note, so called because it produces a discordant sound with other notes of the *raga* and is consequently little used if the *raga* is of a peaceful mood.

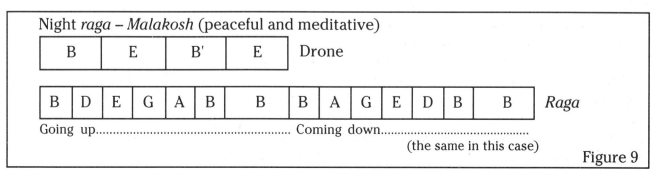

Night *raga* – *Malakosh* (peaceful and meditative)				
B	E	B'	E	Drone

B	D	E	G	A	B	B	B	A	G	E	D	B	B	*Raga*

Going up.. Coming down..
(the same in this case)

Figure 9

A typical performance

The music begins slowly with little rhythmic emphasis with the drone. The soloist then joins in, announcing the character of the *raga* by emphasising the *vadi*, *samvadi* and *anuvadi* notes. In the next section, the music becomes more rhythmic and the tabla player may join in with the *tala*. The speed gradually increases as does the complexity of the improvisations until a final section is reached in which some of the music played before is repeated and an exciting climax reached. Although common, this is only one form which a performance may take. It is clear that experimental use of this kind of music in the classroom can provide only the most basic experience, but ways in which this may be approached are described below.

Playing the tala

Write up one of the *talas* shown in Figure 10 on the board or on a piece of card. The number of boxes which represent the number of basic beats in the *tala* can be counted by the whole class a few times before playing to establish a settled rhythmic feeling. For *Dadra* the class would count: 1 2 3 4 5 6/ 1 2 3 4 5 6.

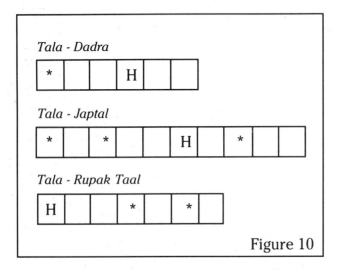

Figure 10

Where there are symbols in the boxes the class should respond. The familiar * signifies clapping but the H symbol is

slightly more complex. This is a gesture, made with the back of the hand towards the audience. It signifies a silent beat and is often accompanied with an inclination of the head as if to say, 'There is the beat which you know about but can't hear'.

Try *Japtal* in the same way. The class should count up to ten before playing this one.

Rupak Taal begins with the gesture of the hand. This should be fairly simple if, initially, a group of children count to keep the rest steadily on the rhythm. If the *tala* is written out on card or on the board, however, the need for counting becomes redundant and the children will begin to feel the rhythm without having to count.

Playing the drone

Although a keyboard is ideal for playing the drone, any pitched instrument can be used. The drone needs to move more slowly than the basic counted pulse. Two, three or four beats to each drone note should give a satisfactory effect. The drone can be practised and then played with a *tala*. Some possible drones are shown in Figure 11.

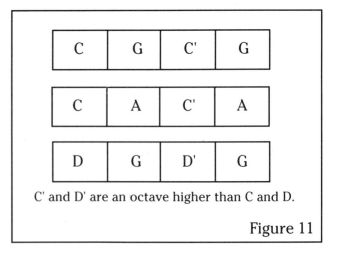

C' and D' are an octave higher than C and D.

Figure 11

Attempting a whole piece

The typical performance as described above contains features which may be impractical in a classroom performance. The complex final section of an improvisation using a *raga* would be hard

Night *raga* – *Malakosh* (peaceful and meditative)

B	E	B'	E	Drone

B	D	E	G	A	B		B	A	G	E	D	B	B	*Raga*

Going up.. Coming down...
(the same in this case)

*		*	*			H			*			*Tala*

1. Play the drone at a steady speed.
2. Improvise on the *raga* in a dreamy style.
3. Improvise on the *raga* in a rhythmic way.
4. Play the *tala* — four beats to each note of the drone.
5. Try to get gradually faster before the end.

Figure 12

to achieve, but this is not essential when simply trying to provide a basic understanding of how the skilled player works. It would be silly to expect a child composing in the European style to approach the intricacies of Bach and Beethoven. On the other hand, there may be children in class who are familiar with Indian classical music and this will be an opportunity for a rich form of sharing. The bare essentials for the performance of a *raga* are set out in Figure 12.

There are a number of useful books which give details of the individual sounds of *ragas*. It is meaningless merely to tell children that a certain *raga* reflects a mood of anger, while another reflects a feeling of loneliness. Invite them to suggest a feeling that they think the notes convey.

Indonesian music

Unlike the music of Africa, the Caribbean and India, Indonesian music has not been assimilated into British culture. Indeed, there are few Indonesian children in the classrooms of Britain compared with those of other ethnic groups. Neil Sorrel, in *Pop, Rock and Ethnic Music in School*, makes the point that it is good for children in a multicultural classroom to unite

unselfconsciously together to investigate a kind of music which is part of none of their cultures. The great beauty of the sound of the gamelan orchestra, together with the social skills needed for a number of children to play together effectively, are

strong arguments for the investigation of this kind of music.

Besides gongs, instruments such as flutes, zithers, xylophones and fiddles are included in the gamelan orchestra. The most visually striking, however, is the gamelan itself, with its gongs which hang on a painted frame, carved with dragons' heads and traditional designs. Because genuine imported gamelans are very expensive, secondary schools have run projects in which gamelans have been built. It is perfectly possible for primary children to play in a gamelan style with the use of chime bars and other classroom instruments. This helps them to appreciate recorded examples of the real thing.

A rhythmic exercise

Start by organising rhythms in a simple way. This will involve the kind of group co-operation which is central to Indonesian music. It can be practised using word rhythms, so let the class stand in a circle and speak the following:

'Now let us/play a/Balinese/rhythm.'
– • • – – • • – • •

This should be repeated four or five times until the rhythm is absolutely secure.

Then divide the class into two and get the children to speak the line in two parts, so that half the class repeats the line and the second half joins in one beat later after the line has been once repeated:

Now let us / play a / Balinese / rhythm
Now let us / play a / Balinese / rhythm
    Now let us / play a / Balinese...

Ask each half to begin their line again when they have spoken it through so that the second part continues one beat behind.

Try this with the children speaking and clapping. When they are confident, try the rhythm again using only clapping.

Next divide the class into three. Ask the first group to speak their line and get the second group to join in after hearing it through once. Let the third group wait until the second group have spoken their line once, then let them begin to speak also on the second beat:

Now let us / play a / Balinese / rhythm.
    Now let us / play a / Balinese /...
      Now let us / play a /...

Again, get the class to practise this by speaking and clapping, and then by clapping. When it is clapped, it will produce a typical interlocking rhythm.

		*			*		*			*			*˙		*
*			*		*			*		*		*			
	*			*		*			*			*		*	
*			*			*		*			*			*	
	*					*			*		*				
		*		*					*						*
			*			*			*			*			*

These can be remembered by children as follows:

(line 1) 1 2 3 1 2 3 1 2 1 2 3 1 2 3 1 2
(line 2) 1 2 3 1 2 1 2 3 1 2 3 1 2 1 2 3
(line 3) 1 2 1 2 3 1 2 1 2 3 1 2 3 1 2 3
(line 4) 1 2 3 1 2 3 1 2 1 2 3 1 2 3 1 2
(line 5) 1 2 3 1 2 3 1 2 3 1 2 3 1 2 1 2
(line 6) 1 2 3 1 2 3 1 2 3 1 2 3 1 2 1 2
(line 7) 1 2 3 1 2 3 1 2 3 1 2 3 1 2 1 2

Figure 13

The Kecak chorus

Taken from the dance dramas based on the *Ramayana*, a traditional epic about the god Rama and his wife, Sita, the Kecak chorus represents a horde of chattering monkeys and the effect, using the syllable 'chak' on each indicated beat, is remarkable. The 'chak' should be pronounced in such a way that the throat is closed on the final 'k', producing what is known as a 'glottal stop'.

The effect of this piece of Balinese music is breathtaking. It is quite feasible for it to be performed by junior children, though the initial 'getting it together' will be a challenge. A suggestion of how the rhythms can be counted is printed below the grid in Figure 13. Take it slowly at first.

Rhythm and melody

The complex textures played by the gamelan orchestra cannot be reproduced in the classroom without considerable knowledge and practice, the attainment of which would be an inappropriate chore. However, it is possible to introduce the basic principles of gamelan music to complement the process of listening to recordings and to help develop a feeling for this music.

In Java two scales are used. The *slendro* is what we would call the 'pentatonic scale' (for example, C D E G A). The *pelog* can also be played on the white notes of the piano (E F G A B C D).

In gamelan music, the largest gongs tend to play the slowest notes and the smaller and most agile instruments play the quick melodies. It is possible to experience the flavour of gamelan playing by inventing a melody on one of the scales and then playing it very slowly on the lowest xylophone, at twice the speed on a middle sized instrument and twice the speed again on a higher-pitched instrument. A suspended cymbal and a gong can play at longer intervals, and chime bars or recorders can play quickly moving decorative figures. Alternatively, an interlocking device can be used. An example is given in Figure 14 overleaf which involves interlocking between the xylophone and the metalophone and between the xylophone and the glockenspiel.

Glockenspiel	CDCD	CDCD	CDCD	CDCD	GAGA	GAGA	GAGA	GAGA	GAGA	GAGA	GAGA	GAGA	CDCD	CDCD	CDCD	CDCD
Xylophone	xG	xA	xG	xA	xG	xA	xG	xG	xB	xB	xG	xG	xA	xA	xG	xC
Metalophone	E	G	F	F	A	B	C	A	G	A	E	F	G	B	D	C
Cymbals				*				*				*				*

In the xylophone part xD means a hit on the second half of the beat. This makes the part interlock with the metalophone.

Music composed by children at Turves Green School, Birmingham. Metalophone tune composed first using Pelog scale.

Figure 14

The glockenspiels play quick notes which continue throughout the piece:

/CDCD/CDCD/CDCD/CDCD/GAGA/ etc.

The metalophone plays on the *first* note of each of the glockenspiels' four-note groups:

/E   /G   /F   /F   /A   / etc.

The xylophone interlocks with the metalophone by playing on the *third* note of each of the glockenspiels' four-note groups:

/   G/   A/   G/   A/   G   /etc.

The interlocking effect between the xylophone and the metalophone is as follows:

/E G /G A /F G /F A /A G / etc.

This piece was made up by a group of children, and makes a convincing gamelan-like sound. However, apart from using a Javanese scale, very little knowledge of gamelan music was needed for its composition.

Sharing cultures

It is to share the feeling which another culture has for music that is most important. To recognise a style is to stand outside and merely to look in, and merely to accept another's musical sounds has little value. It is hoped that by being able to take part, not only in the playing but also in the thinking that, like the little girl who wept for Flora MacDonald and Bonnie Prince Charlie, people of all cultures may recognise in others something of themselves.

136

Chapter 18
The recorder

Long before most of today's orchestral instruments were invented, the recorder was common throughout Europe. The recorder has changed little in form, though the materials from which it is made have undergone great change.

The recorder in school

It was due to Edgar Hunt and Arnold Dolmetsch, who had particular interests in medieval instruments, that the recorder became readily available in this country in the early part of this century. It immediately became popular in schools because until that time there had been no instruments that were as easy to play to a reasonable standard as well as being affordable. The recorder was available at one-thirtieth the price of the cheapest orchestral wind instrument.

As the popularity of the recorder grew, so the teaching of it became generally less effective. There were, of course, excellent teachers of the recorder, but the recorder came, in some quarters, to be regarded almost as a toy. Some teachers even began to learn to play the instrument while they stood in front of their classes, learning with the children whom they were teaching.

This was probably one of the greatest causes of 'wrong-handedness'. When facing a class, the teacher's left hand is on the same side as the children's right hand and this caused many children to take up the wrong-handed playing position. (This is also sometimes seen in conductors who have risen from the ranks of the choir and who beat time in the wrong direction, thus confusing visiting orchestral players.)

Once used to playing wrong-handed, children make all sorts of excuses, such as 'I'm left-handed'. In such a case, they should be told that they are lucky, since the left hand does the most work in the early stages, so there is no excuse for not having their clever hand at the top!

It is not sufficient just to 'know' a few notes to be able to teach. This misguided attitude is sometimes encountered in players of orchestral instruments. Highly qualified on the clarinet, for instance, a player then learns the notes of the flute or oboe, or both, and proceeds to try to teach all three. The matters of technique which relate to the clarinet are well known to them but bad habits develop in their flute or oboe pupils which they are not qualified to diagnose.

Buying a recorder

Recorder playing often starts with the purchase of an instrument. The finest, and most expensive, are made of wood. These are essential to a player who really means to reach a high standard and must be looked after with specialist care. Even the cheapest wooden recorder needs this care if it is not to become a useless tube after six months. The wooden recorder is not suitable for a beginner and should not be in a school set.

Modern school-quality recorders are made of plastic and are much more resilient to damage. They don't need to be oiled, and when they become furred up with dust and condensed breath, they can be swished about in soapy water, rinsed and, after a good shake, played again. They do not mind being left in bright sunlight and, if sat on, there is very little likelihood of damage.

It is unfortunate that there are some 'instruments' which are sold under the name of recorder by non-specialist shops and chain stores. They are often brightly coloured and very attractive to children, but they do not play in tune throughout their compass and should not be bought. The purchase of such an instrument is likely to inhibit a child's progress and will certainly lead to out-of-tune playing in comparison with a properly made recorder.

Purchase through the school

The only place to buy a recorder is from a reputable music shop. Enquiries should be made so that if parents need advice they can be directed to a suitable shop. Perhaps a better way to help, if a large number of sales is likely, is to contact a nationally known company, such as Schott, Boosey and Hawkes or E J Arnold, and to find out the cost of a bulk order. There will always be a discount and the recorders can then be sold through the school with a profit for the school fund. Try to ensure that all the recorders in the school are of the same make, so that they will all play in tune with each other.

Hygiene

If a set of recorders is to be bought for the school, there is one consideration which should be borne in mind. Cleanliness is vital and the use of an antiseptic dip when the recorders are handed back from the players is crucial. Listerine mouth wash has always proved effective, though there are suitable alternatives. A bottle can be kept with the recorders, together with a plastic mug, and a diluted solution used as the recorders are returned to their box. Dipping a recorder to a depth of about one inch is sufficient to remove the danger of passing on infection.

Why consider the recorder?

It has been suggested that to teach the recorder in schools is to force children to learn disciplines which have no relevance to them. This may, of course, be the case with some children although in one school, which had an excellent reputation for music and at which all the first year juniors played the recorder once a week, it was noted that there was a very high percentage attendance at after-school musical activities, and music was generally regarded as part of life by about 200 out of the 280 on roll. The teacher in charge of music ascribed this enthusiasm to early experience of recorder playing.

The best reason for teachers knowing about the recorder is because in the schools of our country there are literally thousands of recorders. If a proper approach is made to their use, then great value can be obtained. If the recorder is badly taught, the children gain little or nothing and the use of the instrument is reduced to the level of something learned by rote to make a good impression at a festival.

Who should play?

Selection of the children whom one thinks will be competent is usually successful, but this defeats the object of giving an opportunity to the widest possible range of children. If, once a child has joined the group, the teacher insists on standards of effort which causes them to de-select themselves, nothing is lost, but the satisfaction of seeing an unlikely child succeed and stick is considerable.

Ask the children who would like to play the recorder. In the infant school, and the first year of the junior age range, almost everyone will volunteer. Later on there will be fewer applicants because unfortunately it will probably have been established that the recorder is for girls and thus no self-respecting boy would risk the consequent taunts.

This situation can be remedied in the same way that little girls who refuse to use a saw and who pass the tool to a boy to use can be encouraged. One of the best ways of doing this is to present adult role models. Just as you would give children the opportunity to see women sawing a piece of wood or wiring a plug, so you should present men playing recorders. In one school where playing the violin was thought of as a girls' occupation, an extremely hearty, football-playing *and* violin-playing Welshman joined the staff.The applicants to play the violin became equally representative of both sexes within six months.

Choosing music

There are many books available from which a good start can be made with the help of an informed teacher. Books which contain pop songs should be avoided for the beginner because of their awkward rhythms. Various beginner books are listed in the Resources section on page 179 and these include plenty of good tunes.

Using notation

An early approach to teaching the recorder involved playing from letters rather than notes. However, it was found that using letter names for notes tended to discourage children from sight-reading in the early stages. When it is clear that children are playing from the *positions* of notes on the stave, the names of the notes can be introduced as musical knowledge, but not as cues to finger positions. It is far better to start with the first note in the book and demonstrate the fingering and then make sure that it is copied. A method for reading rhythm, 'keywords', is suggested in the Chapter 20, page 158 and, with the help of this, playing at sight can take place from the outset and new notes can be added by the same process. If letter names for notes are taught first, the process, as a child reads from music, is as follows: see a note; think the letter; think the fingering of that letter; play. Surely the following is preferable: see the note; think the fingering; play.

Many children say they cannot play without the letters written in below the notes. This, of course, will prevent them from ever bothering to look properly at the position of the note which thus becomes redundant. Some teachers find that the 'festival piece' will not be ready unless the letters are written in. Once this is done, however, the children will always want this

prompt. This will not arise if from the start letter names of notes are not mentioned.

The first lesson

A first recorder lesson might run as follows. This is designed to get right at the outset the many things which will otherwise prevent progress from being made.

Give out the recorders to the children. Hold one up in your left hand, standing with your back turned to the class. Ask the children to hold their recorders in the same hand and hold them up.

Tell the children to 'put the mouthpiece on your chin'. (This prevents blowing while positional instructions are being given.) The children should now be holding the recorder in the left hand with the mouthpiece on the chin.

Keeping your back to the class, hold up your right hand and ask the children to do the same. Turn to the class and say, 'Put your little finger on the joint between the two bottom holes.' Go round the class to check that this has been done. Unless in use to play the bottom note, the little finger should always rest in this position. By this means the right-hand fingers will have a point of reference and fall cleanly on to the holes below them.

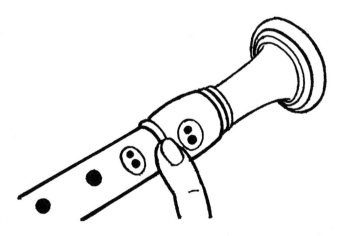

Say to the children, 'Put three fingers of the left hand on the top three holes so that they are flat and press; if you look at your fingers you will see little ring marks on the pads of your fingers.'

By this means it is possible to see that the fingers are in the right position. Horseshoe shapes on the finger pads indicate that the hole was not covered properly. When the three fingers are in a good position, then tell them to feel with the thumb for the thumb hole.

When a child is about to put a recorder in her mouth she sees only one hole, the thumb hole, and often this is the first to be covered. It is a mistake to put the thumb on first as the fingers may then have to reach for their holes if an extreme position has been adopted by the thumb. The thumb has a much larger pad and can make a compromise; it fits where it touches. The fingers, with their much smaller pads, cannot make this compromise, so it is important to get the fingers comfortable, then place the thumb in position. This procedure will prevent the squeaks which are usually caused by leaking holes. It is often thought that these squeaks are caused by lower-down fingers not covering the holes properly. Nine times out of ten this squeaking is caused by the left-hand index finger leaking, while the child concentrates on reaching the bottom holes, but if the left-hand fingers take up a good position from the outset, this rarely happens.

Tell the children to replace the recorder on the chin, the right-hand little finger on the bottom joint and three fingers and the thumb of the left hand in place. Then tell the children to remove two fingers so that the recorder is held between finger and thumb. This first note can now be sounded, but it should be emphasised that the recorder is never blown. A gentle sigh (taaaaa) is all that is required and the children should try to make a quiet sound. Over-blowing is another cause of squeaks, but a good example and insistence on a gentle sigh can remove this at the outset.

Go round the class. Let each child try separately to sound the note while you check all the above points. Never let anyone get away with using the wrong hand or playing without the little finger on the joint.

Sight-reading from day one

The note which is produced by the left-hand index finger and thumb (not forgetting the little finger which rests on the lowest joint!) is written in notation as in Figure 1. Let the children prepare the rhythm by speaking and clapping, then play it on the recorder.

A tune with a new note, using two fingers and the thumb of the left hand, can then be attempted using the same rhythm, as in Figure 2.

No mention of note names has been made, but the written notes 'mean' the fingerings which produce the appropriate sounds. Let the children try singing what is written, though of course the singing will sound at a lower pitch than that of the recorder. At first the notes can be sung after playing but there is no reason why, after some experience, the first note should not be given and the children asked to try to sing the whole line of simple music. To set out to teach a group to sing from music

may seem a rather extreme objective, yet it is surprising how well this can work when included in recorder sessions. In this context, sight-singing seems just 'something we sometimes do at recorder lessons' and is in no way intimidating.

A useful listening activity

Once these first two notes are learned, a useful listening game can be included in the lesson. Show the children what note you are going to start on, then turn your back on the class and play a three note phrase, as in Figure 3.

Ask the children to copy the sound. Very soon they will be able to reproduce exactly what is played. It is important, especially as you introduce more notes, that you try to start the next phrase on the last note played. Finding a different note to start a phrase is a considerable quantum leap for a child.

Juniors in Y5 and Y6 have been known to manage quite involved phrases and pick up the new note with surprising skill. This is, of course, the beginning of using the

Figure 1

Figure 2

Figure 3

recorder for composition. Initially, the children simply hear a phrase and copy it, but in doing so they gradually develop an ability to hear a melody in the head and to copy that. Once the fingers can react to a sound and sight-reading has become, to some extent, established, encourage the children to try to write their tunes down and create illuminated manuscripts to decorate classroom walls.

Improvising

In the past children learning an instrument would have been criticised for 'playing by ear'. In fact, they should be encouraged to do so and if a tune is liked they should be encouraged to 'find' it on the recorder.

When a chord sequence is being used (see Chapter 11), a tune or an ostinato may be added using the recorder in the same way as is suggested when employing a glockenspiel. It is important that playing an instrument should not be seen exclusively in terms of reproducing tunes composed by someone else, but also as a means by which one's own musical thoughts can be expressed.

The order in which notes are learned will depend largely upon the book which is used, but these are generally those played only using the left hand. If the first three learned are B, A and G (Figure 4), perfectly acceptable tunes using these notes can be written by children for the group to play. These notes are additionally useful in composition since they are part of a pentatonic scale starting on G (see Chapter

11), so the recorder can be added to the classroom instruments suggested for that activity and take a significant role in composition. For this reason, and because the bottom D and E are straightforward fingerings, it is suggested that these notes are added to the first three, thus completing the whole pentatonic scale on G, though not in actual scale order.

Introducing recorders of different sizes

Once the children's hands are big enough to manage the treble or tenor recorders, playing in parts could be developed. However, a problem might develop which could reduce the effectiveness of the group. The best players will undoubtedly desire a larger instrument and want to move to the treble or tenor, thus weakening the quality of descant playing.

Tenor recorders

Players who are beginning to struggle as descant playing becomes more demanding can be transferred to the tenor recorder, providing their hands are large enough. In such a case, enthusiasm can often be rekindled. One little girl took a school tenor recorder home one Friday, quite unable to reach the holes but returned on the following Monday able to do so. Her family must have suffered a good deal as it was clear that she had practised all weekend, but the availability of this new and exciting instrument, which used the same fingerings as the descant, gave her new drive, and she continued with it until she left for the local secondary school.

In part playing, the music for the tenor recorder is much simpler than that for descant recorders playing the main melody. This can be an additional encouragement for the child for whom playing the melody is getting hard.

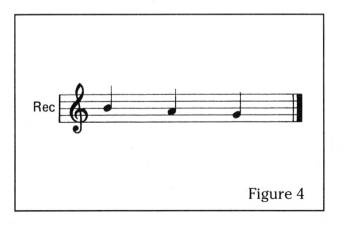

Figure 4

Treble recorders

The difficulties encountered by those transferring to the treble, which has different fingering, are usually surmounted by the most able players. It is important to insist that they sometimes play descant so that the encouragement that they can give to the less able by playing with them is not lost.

Group playing

There is much music available for descant, treble and tenor recorders: considerable pleasure can be gained by the group from playing as a consort. There is also opportunity for children to make up parts in composing their own pieces.

This happy situation is far removed from the first faltering steps when the recorder is rested on the chin while a good playing position is developed. If the practice of playing from notes and not letters is insisted upon and a proper playing posture cultivated, there is no reason why such competency should not be reached. The introduction of treble and tenor should perhaps wait until Y5, Y6 or Y7, but a long-term view and the provision of encouraging and stimulating material will make this possible.

A word of warning

There is one consideration which must be emphasised from day one and rigorously enforced throughout the school.

No child must *ever* walk while playing a recorder or, for that matter, walk with the recorder in his mouth. In a collision a few smashed teeth are negligible compared with the horrifying and permanent injury which can be caused by someone running into the end of a recorder which is being played.

If this dangerous act is seen, confiscate the recorder immediately. If it is owned by the child, ask the parent to collect it. The explanation has never failed to convince a parent that the teacher has acted correctly. If the recorder is owned by the school, withdraw its use for a week; all recorder players *must* see that this rule is kept without question.

Chapter 19
Orchestral instruments

The incidence of orchestral instrumental lessons in primary schools varies greatly from area to area. It is usually assumed that secondary schools are the breeding grounds from which the excellent county youth orchestras and bands grow; this is largely true, but many of these musicians began playing at primary schools.

The violin, 'cello, flute, clarinet and trumpet are most commonly seen at this age range, although the viola, tenor horn and euphonium are perfectly possible. The French horn has also been successfully learned in junior schools, but is so very expensive that its use at this level is relatively rare.

Brass instruments are probably the most inviting from a financial point of view because a skilled trumpet player will be able to teach trumpet, cornet, tenor horn and euphonium and thus be more economical for a school or local authority to employ. The system of fingering and the mouthpiece technique are similar in these four brass instruments which is why a trumpet teacher can provide effective lessons on other instruments. Most other brass instruments share this system of playing which is why a bandmaster, unlike an orchestral conductor, can give lessons to a whole band. Only the trombone, with its slide instead of valves, and the French horn use different systems of note-making.

A number of primary children may play the violin. The violin is relatively cheap to buy, but another specialist usually needs to be called upon if lessons on the 'cello are to be given.

The most successful school instrumental lessons take place in schools which have a positive attitude towards music and where care of instruments is understood and provision for practice made. A teacher who is in charge of music ought to be able to set up and oversee practice, change a broken string, tune a stringed instrument and free a brass instrument's stuck valve. There is also a small matter of making sure that the peripatetic music teacher has a place in the staff room, is made welcome and gets a cup of tea.

Co-operation with visiting teachers

If an instrumental group is to play in assembly, the instrumental teacher's advice should be sought concerning what notes the pupils can play or ought to be asked to play. Many visiting teachers are only too glad to provide a playable and effective line and to practise it with the players concerned. Teaching around the schools can be a lonely business and to know that one's efforts are appreciated and one's help valued makes a great deal of difference.

Taking care of instruments

The general class teacher has an important part to play. Instruments will be brought to school and unless a secure place for them is found by the headteacher or the school secretary, it is likely that they will need to be kept in a safe place in the classroom.

Stringed instruments

For stringed instruments, a high shelf, a secure cupboard or an out-of-the-way table can be useful. The stock cupboard is not a good idea, as children may pass in and out: one kick from a careless passer-by may result in someone with sufficient skill having to spend fifteen minutes replacing the bridge or re-setting the sound post.

Since violins and 'cellos are glued together, close contact with heating pipes is disastrous. It is best to avoid leaving stringed instruments near a window as the sun could easily raise their temperature to dangerous levels.

Woodwind instruments

This same problem of heat applies to the woodwind instruments. The pads – those small cushions under the keys which are pressed down by the fingers – are made to fit exactly with the help of a kind of hard glue which can be softened by heat to allow the pad to take up the shape complementary to the hole which it covers. If warmed, the pad may shift and when cool again it may develop a leak which could make the instrument temporarily unplayable. The fact that the visiting instrumental teacher could put this right in two minutes with the help of a cigarette lighter is no consolation to the child who is deprived of the use of the instrument for a week. Parents have been known to rush off to a music shop in panic and be charged a significant sum which could have been avoided with proper care. The flute, which has a mass of these pads, is most vulnerable to this heat threat since it is invariably made of metal and thus conducts heat very easily.

The clarinet has its own personal perils, related to the actual handling of the instrument. When a player is putting her instrument together, a lever of one piece must come together with a similar lever on the other. If care is not exercised, it is too easy to crush one lever against the other which results in bending or breakage.

The most frequently seen damage to both clarinets and oboes occurs when a classmate says, 'Let's have a go'. If the child takes the instrument and then, in an effort to see his fingers, leans the mouthpiece towards him, the reed inevitably touches his chest, becomes entangled in his pullover, and splits.

Brass instruments

Brass instruments are relatively hardy which may account for their popularity with the armed forces. There are, however, a few rules which need to be observed and which the class teacher needs to know. The mouthpiece is separate from the

instrument, with its special place in the instrument case. While it is fairly difficult to lose a whole trumpet, it is all too easy to lose a mouthpiece. These are extremely expensive and their absence renders the instrument useless. When an instrument case is passed into the care of a teacher, she should immediately check that the mouthpiece is with its instrument. Much time can be wasted in trying to find out who has been into the cupboard and removed a mouthpiece which a child has actually left at home.

It may be discovered that a valve – one of the keys which the fingers press down to change notes – has stuck. These can be unscrewed at the top and gently eased out. A squirt of valve oil will cure the trouble, though good old-fashioned spit is as good as anything. No other kind of oil is acceptable. A problem can arise when the valve is replaced in the instrument. It can

only fit properly in one position because there is a lug on the valve which must be located in a slot on the inside of the cylinder. If the valve is forced in without lug and slot coming together, no amount of oil will coax it out again, the piston will jam and an expert will have to be called in. Brute force can often result in permanent damage. Valves should be removed only one at a time. This ensures that they are returned to their own position. They are all different, and if replaced in the wrong order, the instrument will not play. In such a case, a number of permutations have to be tried in the presence of someone who can actually tell whether the instrument is working or not. If valves are numbered, and many are, note their positions before removal.

Listening to instruments

Musical instruments hold a considerable attraction for children and if 'real' experience can be provided, most of them will find the experience both relevant and interesting.

This can be achieved by inviting into school a musician who will let the children hear, handle and even attempt to make sounds from an instrument. Musicians often tend to be good communicators and enjoyable sessions for the whole school can be arranged. When a visiting player, who is not accustomed to talking to children, is invited to come and demonstrate his instrument, you can help by arranging for there to be a question-and-answer session and, having discussed the session with the proposed visitor, judge how much help in this direction is required.

When inviting those who do not have the gift of communicating with children, there is a danger that they will opt to play a few sonatas which are quite outside the children's experience. Some material of this sort should be included, but the ability to play tunes from television advertisements and the signature tunes of soap operas is essential. It is this kind of material which bridges the gap between the children's experience and the music which demonstrates the instrument's capabilities.

County instrumental music teachers tend to be very good at this kind of thing, especially since they are often required to have teaching qualifications. Some authorities have encouraged their teacher/players to form groups which tour schools and these have been much enjoyed.

Some years ago, a Birmingham group spiced their performance by developing characters for the players. One apparently kept falling asleep and another was the proverbial 'naughty boy' and, between bursts of virtuoso playing, the children were kept in fits of laughter at the antics of a group who clearly enjoyed the performance as much as the children. The attitude to music as a solemn and serious study, which was fostered by music teachers of an earlier generation, was probably one of the most damaging influences which any art form has inflicted upon itself.

Using 'local' talent

Children who are fairly skilled players should be encouraged to demonstrate their instruments in whatever way is both possible and appropriate. If it is possible to form some kind of band, avoid the temptation to make an end-of-term concert the first priority. The first priority should be to bring the use of instruments into school life, for example, by letting the children play the daily hymn or song at assembly. It is important to let children see that such playing is not an elitist activity. For this reason the presence of the band in assemblies is more important than its function of enhancing the school's public image.

The difficulties which stand in the way of some children playing often include a lack of parental support, and even actual opposition to practising at home. There are many things in education which, though undesirable, can never be totally mended. It is necessary to summon up the optimism and courage to make the offer of starting up a band. The degree of acceptance relies upon too many imponderables for you to be able to forecast the response.

The instruments

There are four families of instruments. Some produce sound by drawing a bow across a string (the string family); some are blown and were, traditionally at least, made of wood (the woodwind family); some are blown and are made of brass (the brass family); and some are hit (the percussion family).

Strings

It is often assumed that the four members of the string section – the violin, the viola, the 'cello (violincello) and the double bass – are basically the same instruments but of different sizes. This is not the case; the double bass is a much older instrument than the rest and a member of a quite different instrument family.

Double bass

The double bass is a viol, the family of stringed instruments in use before the advent of the violin and its bigger sisters. Its ancestors first appeared in the fifteenth century. Originally larger with six strings and known as the violone, it was modified to become a practical fourth member of the orchestral string section. Its strings are, however, tuned four notes apart instead of the five in the true violin and its shoulders are more sloping than those of the 'cello. It is also thicker from front to back and produces a more reedy and penetrating tone than the smooth-sounding violins.

There is a further consideration which has caused the double bass to persist in place of a theoretically possible bass violin. The player simply could not reach over the shoulders of a huge violin without the kind of damaging strain which, as it is, afflicts many orchestral players. Furthermore, the tone of such an instrument, for some were made, proved too gentle and lacking in the 'bite' which was demanded by composers. Consequently the modernised violone is the accepted bass stringed instrument of the orchestra.

Violin, viola and 'cello

The violin, viola and 'cello are all members of the violin family which began to take over in popularity in the early seventeenth century. The violin has never been improved upon since those times when the great Italian masters of the art of violin-making, such as Stradivarius and Guarneri, were working in Cremona. There have been improvements in details such as chin rests and strings, but little else has changed and many of those old instruments are still played today.

The violoncello is commonly known as the 'cello which explains the apostrophe which is part of the correct spelling.

Woodwinds

Flute

As far as the method of blowing is concerned, the flute is probably the oldest of the woodwind instruments. The sound is produced by blowing across a hole which might have originally been the end of a bone or a cleanly cut hollow plant stem.

Over the last 200 years, the fingering of the instrument has changed beyond recognition. At first there was one single key at the bottom end of the instrument, but more were added as time went on. Theobald Boehm invented the modern system in 1832 in order to enable players to manage musical passages which were virtually impossible on the existing instrument, and pioneered the use of precious metals instead of the traditional wood. Instruments of 'bakelite'-type materials were made for use in the hot climates endured by the British Army in India.

Piccolo

Piccolo, in translation, means 'little'. This is because English usage has been based on the belief that this was the Italian name for the instrument. In fact the Italian name is *flauto piccolo* which means 'the little flute', and that is exactly what it is. It can play the highest practical note in the orchestra and can be heard doing so even when the rest of the band are playing fortissimo. It has been tried as a starter instrument in schools, but any child who has already played the flute is likely to be disappointed. There is a great tendency to force the tone, which is difficult to develop, and the cost of the instrument is as much as a full-sized flute.

Oboe

The oboe uses a double reed, two pieces of reed bound together which allow air to pass between them. The construction was originally of wood, though successful instruments have been made of composite materials; Rossini owned an instrument made of ivory (now in the Victoria and Albert Museum's Musical Instrument Gallery in London). The 'back pressure' required to make the instrument sound makes some authorities doubtful if the instrument is suitable to be learned by children under 14. A soft reed is required to make the instrument sound more easily, though this produces a coarse tone and is thought by some to encourage bad practice.

Cor anglais

The cor anglais is neither a horn (cor), nor English, though it is often called the 'English horn'. It is like a large oboe and has a rich and magical sound.

Clarinet

The clarinet is a transposing instrument. This means that when the fingering of C is played on the most commonly seen B♭ instrument, B♭ sounds. Clarinets are available in several keys, the next most common of which is the clarinet in A which produces an A when C is fingered. The different kinds of clarinets are retained because the tone qualities are so different. The A clarinet has a marvellously dark quality, while the C clarinet has a stronger and more cutting tone than the B♭ instrument. The E♭ clarinet used in military bands can positively scream. All use a single reed in common with the bass clarinet, which looks like an emaciated saxophone but has a wonderfully rich sound. The contra bass clarinet, of which very few exist, is hardly more than an amusing curiosity.

Bassoon

The bassoon makes its sounds using a double reed similar to that of the oboe. First recorded in the fifteenth century, though with a different system of fingering, it came to be treated as the fool of the orchestra and, in the nineteenth century, sank to the level of being the prop of music hall funny men. It is unlikely that a primary child would be big enough to take up this instrument and the extremely high cost has always prevented it from being as popular with young players as the rest of the woodwinds. The contra bassoon, the bassoon's bigger brother, can play the lowest notes possible in the orchestra.

Brass

It is tempting to deal with the brass in one paragraph since they all use the principle of the 'harmonic series', that is, they can play several notes on one length of tubing. The sizes and shapes of the various instruments differ greatly, thus producing different tone qualities.

Trumpet

The trumpet has a narrow bore, like the trombone, so despite the different method of playing, these two are closely related.

Cornet

The cornet resembles the trumpet but has a wider bore and produces a sweeter sound. This method of construction is echoed in the brass band instruments of tenor horn, baritone horn and bombardons, all of which are of tuba shape, though of different sizes.

French horn

The French horn, which looks as if it has been wound into a circle, can produce more notes of the harmonic series (more notes without moving the fingers) than any other member of the brass family. This is because of the shape of the tubing and of the mouthpiece which is long and narrow. The fingering system of this instrument is different from the other 'valved' instruments and a good ear is required if one is to be a successful player. The horn, as it is known, is likely to be very expensive and this, no doubt, accounts for its rarity. It has been successfully learned in a junior school but, as the player had already shown promise on the tenor horn and descant and treble recorders, he clearly began lessons with an advantage.

Trombone

The trombone comes in two sizes, tenor and bass. It makes its notes with the help of a slide which is pushed in and out. It is the most powerful instrument in the orchestra.

Tuba

The tuba is not likely to be found in junior schools. The orchestral tuba is a transposing instrument in F and forms the bass part of the brass section.

Euphonium

The euphonium is a middle-sized tuba of the same dimensions as the baritone horn but with a wider bore. It has a miraculously vocal quality and is a favourite solo instrument in the brass band, being capable of incredible agility.

Percussion

The family of percussion instruments is so varied that one can hardly say more than that they are all played by hitting, or sometimes scraping. The most common percussion instruments are described below.

Bass drum and side drum

The bass drum is the largest drum in the band or orchestra, while the side drum (or snare drum) is the smallest free-standing drum in the orchestra. Only the upturned face is played, the lower being covered by a 'snare' of gut or wire. When a rapid pattern of rhythm or a roll is played, the snare vibrates against the lower skin, accentuating the effect.

Timpani

The timpani, or kettle drums, are large drums, two to five in number which can be tuned. They provide bass notes as required or thunderous effects. Modern 'timps' can be retuned very quickly with a foot pedal. The player is a specialist.

Glockenspiel and xylophone

Orchestral glockenspiels and xylophones are very similar to those instruments frequently found in the classroom, although they are larger and more resonant. The glockenspiels have metal bars while the xylophone's bars are made of wood.

Cymbals

The cymbals can either be clashed or struck with a stick. If they are clashed, they

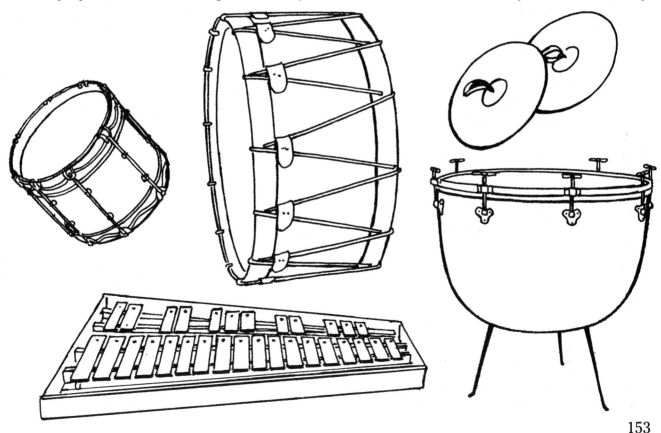

have a strap for each of the player's hands. If the cymbal is struck, it is usually suspended on a stand. Sometimes loose rivets are set in the surface of the cymbal which chatter when the cymbal is struck, producing a hissing sound.

They can also be played with wire brushes. Wire brushes, however, are dangerous, especially those which can be retracted into the handle. Care should be exercised when being used by primary children because it is possible to pierce the hand when releasing the brush from the handle.

Castanets

The orchestral version of the castanets sounds like the Spanish traditional instrument, but they are mounted on a handle to enable them to be quickly picked up and put down.

Whip

The whip is not a whip in the normal sense, but two pieces of wood, hinged at one end with handles centrally on each. The flat faces are brought together sharply, producing a whip-like sound.

Claves

Claves are two rods of exceptionally hard wood which together produce an almost metallic 'clink'.

Wood blocks and temple blocks

Wood blocks are box-like instruments of various sizes which produce a hollow sound. Temple blocks resemble (and originally probably were!) skulls. They produce a sound similar to that of the wood blocks, but of differing pitches depending upon their size and volume.

Tubular bells, triangle, tambourine and maracas

Tubular bells are played with mallets.

Triangle, tambourine and maracas are all familiar in both orchestra and school. The maracas were originally large seed-heads which rattled when the seeds became ripe.

Chapter 20
Stock cupboard of music activities

Some years ago I had the job of clearing out the stock room of a teacher of many years whose room I was to take over. It would have been easy to throw away all those bits and pieces which had, for years, been brought out, used and returned to the cupboard. There was a box of coloured lumps of glass, like huge gemstones, which had been brought back from a visit to a glass factory. There were several flags of different nations and jam jars and several balls of brightly coloured wool. There were some fossils, a pond dipping net (torn) and several pieces of drift wood – for all the world like the earthly remains of a teaching career!

This chapter is rather like that cupboard – a collection of dip-in ideas and activities. A fossil has its uses in the reception year and will still be valuable in year ten, and though some indication of the age and stage at which the various activities and ideas might be employed is given, teachers are invited to rummage through and to select what they may think useful. The first section suggests a variety of games relating to aspects of music, and they are mostly concerned with listening and playing.

Section 1: Listening and playing games

The dragon's gold

This game encourages attentive listening and develops control of simple instruments. It has been used successfully with children up to year four and even older children can play it in a small group.

A pile of classroom instruments of the sort which make a sound when moved carelessly – tambourine, maracas – are placed in the middle of a circle of children. One child is chosen to be the 'dragon' and he stands next to the pile. The dragon is then blindfolded – a dragon mask adds interest to the game, though mere blindfolding will do.

The instruments are the dragon's hoard of treasure and once he is on guard, the teacher points to one child who creeps out and tries to steal an instrument. The dragon listens carefully and if he can point to the thief, the thief becomes the new dragon.

The tambourine race

This game helps to develop the ability to control instruments. It can be used from the reception year, throughout the entire school age range and even with in-service courses to settle the group and to introduce the subject matter.

Divide the group into two equal teams, facing one another. (If there is an odd number, one child can be the 'winning post'.) Each team is then given a tambourine. On the word GO, the tambourines are passed from one end of each team to the other. The team that gets its tambourine to the winning post first is the winner, but this must be done in complete silence. If an instrument makes a rattle, it must go back two places. To speak can be counted as making a sound, which makes this good practice in remaining silent. The teacher makes sure the rules are enforced.

Name rhythms

The use of 'Name rhythms' is suitable from the reception year onwards.

Use the children's names to provide practice in simple rhythmic patterns. Choose a child's name and clap it, for example:

Niluka Sujeevani, Niluka Sujeevani etc.

When the children think that they know whose name it is, they should signal that they know by joining in with the clapping and then you can ask them to say the name.

An extension of this game is rather like Peg Leg Pete (see page 25), though in this case the child who knocks taps out his name, which has to be recognised from the rhythm.

As the children's skill increases, they can devise very simple compositions called 'Ourselves' or 'Us'. This might involve a small group of children putting their name rhythms together and making a rhythmic piece. Instruments can be added and pitched notes can also be included.

LOX (Listening noughts and crosses)

Draw a large noughts and crosses grid on a piece of A4 paper. In each of the nine spaces, draw or stick on a picture of a different classroom instrument – for example, drum, tambourine, triangle, rhythm sticks, jingles, maracas, Indian bells, guiro and bells. Make a copy for each player or team of players. The players (or teams) take it in turn to signal moves by playing the instrument shown in the chosen space. The instruments need to be hidden behind a screen or, if there are two sets of each, each player or team can have a set and be situated out of sight of each other. Each team has counters with either noughts or crosses on them and the moves of both teams are made as the game progresses. Children watching can have a sheet and counters and act as referees for the game.

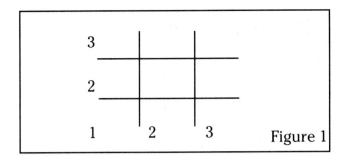

Figure 1

A similar noughts and crosses grid with number coordinates can be used for very simple grid referencing (see Figure 1). The moves are signalled by taps on an instrument – Eastings before Northings – thus combining a listening activity with a useful mathematical principle.

Word rhythms of pictures, drawn or stuck in the spaces, can also be tapped out to signal moves – combine harvester, intercity train etc.

Still yet another variation of the noughts and crosses grid is that it can be marked with rhythms in standard musical notation and these rhythms used to communicate the position of a move (see Figure 2).

Figure 2

The clap click game

This is a simple game using sounds made with different parts of the body. It can be modified to suit any age range from year one to year seven. A series of numbers are written on the chalkboard or on a large piece of card, such as:

1 2 2 3 4 1 2 3

The children speak the numbers rhythmically as the teacher points to them until the whole class can get it completely right.

Next sounds are substituted for the numbers: 'Clap instead of saying 1. Speak all the rest.'

The class practises this, then the teacher says, 'Now we will add a finger click instead of saying 2.'

The class does so, still speaking 3 and 4.

A further sound is added and the process repeated. When all the numbers are turned into sounds, the class can be divided in half and a competition held to see which half can perform better.

This game can be used in preparation for the activities leading to the use of polyrhythms (Chapter 15) and to the use of rhythm grids.

In the early years the following will suffice:

1 2 3 1 2 2 3 1

but a more challenging series of numbers, played at a lively speed, can be used to stretch top juniors, not to mention teachers on in-service courses.

The tick tock game

This game has been used throughout the primary age range and, for an extremely simple idea, it makes considerable demands.

All one needs is a two-tone block and a beater. The game can either be played so that the players can see the instrument or with the block hidden behind a screen. Call the two sounds 'tick' and 'tock'. The lower of the two is 'tock'.

The game follows on from 'say what I say' and 'clap what I say activities'. Keeping a steady four-beat pattern in mind, play the following:

1	2	3	4
Tock	Tick, tick	Tock	Tick

The children respond by saying the words rhythmically. Try other rhythms, for example:

157

1	2	3	4
Tick, tick	Tick, tick	Tock	Tock

or:

1	2	3	4
Tock, tock	Tock, tock	Tick	Tick

The wide spacings are indications that a sound takes up one whole beat; two sounds close together share the same beat. The sound that falls on the beat is indicated by a capital letter.

The children must start as soon as you have finished and you must start the second pattern as soon as they have finished so that there is a steady rhythmic flow.

This is an excellent starter to a lesson with children who have had some practice at 'echo' work (see page 37). If there are a number of instruments available which can make a 'tick tock' sound, then a group can play the game, taking it in turns to speak rhythms which have to be played. Finally, the game can be played as a competition with the class divided into two or more teams.

Rhythm tag

This is a boisterous game for juniors which needs to be played in the hall. The required pieces of musical equipment are a wood block and a drum. A player of each stands at either end of the hall.

The drummer begins to play a simple rhythm, for example: 'Brown paper, brown paper... etc.'

The wood block player joins in with a different rhythm: 'Silver paper, silver paper... etc.'

Two catchers are chosen and they have to 'tag' the remaining members of the class. One catcher sends those he tags to the drummer's end of the hall where they have to join in with the drum rhythm by clapping. The other chaser tags children who are sent to play with the wood block player. The winner is the catcher with the most players in his band.

This game should be played in vocal silence, though inevitably there will be a good deal of thumping about the floor.

Section 2: Keywords

An approach to the understanding of rhythmic notation

Keywords are simply words which provide a key to unlock most of the mysteries of rhythmic notation. There are those who insist that musical notation has no place in school. 'This kind of information has no relevance to children's needs and experience!' But whatever education is, it is not something which deals in exclusions and since the ability to read and write rhythmic notation is a large part of musical literacy, a convincing argument that understanding notation is a 'bad thing' would be hard to sustain. Compare the situation with another subject by replacing the word 'music' with 'mathematics'.

At the same time the meaningless teaching of note values to all children is a waste of their time and, incidentally, has little to do with music as it has correctly come to be perceived. There may, however, come a moment when it is clear that an ability to read and write standard notation is not merely relevant but desirable, and it is hoped that this section will provide an approach for answering this.

If word rhythms have been used to remind children of what they are to play, and physical skills have been built up to make it possible for them to do so, then words, related to common groupings of rhythmic values, can be used to link the meanings of symbols to their appearance.

The simplest body rhythm is that produced by walking, and the most common symbol in musical notation is the 'crotchet' (♩).

The fact that it is called a crotchet has no value. The Americans call it a quarter note, though that is of equally little assistance in the actual use of the symbol because one does not usually meet the note of which it is one-fourth part until later in musical life. If, on the other hand, a crotchet is given a keyword which indicates how it really sounds, then the symbol will immediately remind a child of what he needs to play. Consider the following:

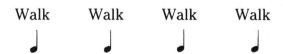

Walk   Walk   Walk   Walk

If, in the early stages of learning about notation, the crotchet is called a 'walk', then the word itself can provide a rhythm that will guide the playing of a phrase.

In one book, two quavers (♫) were described as two halfpennies which equalled one penny (the crotchet). The relationship was clear, but this did not enable the child to sense the rhythmic implications. That is why the keyword for two quavers is 'running':

Walk Run-ning   Run-ning Walk

Following this kind of thinking, the minim (♩), which lasts the same length of time as two crotchets, has been given many names – stride, stretch and reach – but perhaps 'stand' is the most logical. Of course, teachers can invent their own set of keywords – those mentioned here are only those which have, over the years, been found useful by the author.

Here is a rhythmic phrase:

How much simpler it seems when word rhythms are applied to its notes:

| 1 | 2 | 3 4 / 1 | | 2 | 3 4 |
| Walk | Walk | Stand | Run-ning | Walk | Stand |

Simple values

The values which have been discussed so far can be divided by two. 'Sta-nd' can be split into two 'walks' and a 'walk' can become 'running', which implies two little beats. The values listed below are called 'simple' values and they qualify for this title because they can be divided by two. Compound rhythms naturally split into three sub-beats and that will become clear when compound values are discussed.

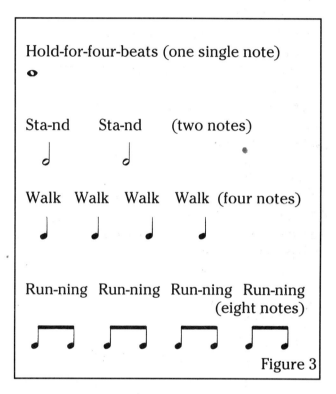

Hold-for-four-beats (one single note)

Sta-nd   Sta-nd   (two notes)

Walk Walk Walk Walk (four notes)

Run-ning Run-ning Run-ning Run-ning (eight notes)

Figure 3

The basic simple notation symbols are shown in Figure 3.

Dotted notes

A dot placed after a note causes it to sound for half as long again as it would have without the dot. Thus:

♩. takes up the same time as ♩ + ♪

This 'dotted minim' (or dotted sta-nd) can be given the keyword 'hold-for-three'. Speak the following keywords:

Walk running walk walk hold-for-three walk

walk walk walk walk hold-for-four-beats.

The rhythms, if written in standard notation, would look like this:

Any note can be dotted and when it is, it is usually followed by a short note. This is because the dotted note has taken up extra time space and there is proportionately less left. Consider the time space taken up by four 'walks':

If the first is dotted, the following note has to 'shrink' in order to fit in to the rhythm.

The dotted note and its shorter companion can here be expressed by the keyword 'limping'. The rhythm would be spoken like this:

```
1   2        3      4
Lim- ping   Walk   Walk
```

Say and clap this a number of times and then try saying and clapping the following example from standard notation.

If a walk can be dotted, then a dot can be placed in a pair of quavers which, you remember, use the keyword 'run-ning'. The same adjustment of the second note has to take place and a useful keyword for this is 'ho-bble'.

Here is a rhythm of a well-known infant song in keywords:

Ho-bble ho-bble walk walk
Ho-bble ho-bble sta-nd

Walk ho-bble walk walk
Ho-bble ho-bble sta-nd

Can you identify it? (The name of the rhyme is given on page 162). The notation would have been written out as follows:

There is one more 'simple time' keyword which may be useful. It is based on the time space taken up by a 'walk'. Standard notation would look like this; the keywords are printed below:

Walk run-ning   run-ning-fas-ter walk

A list of all the keywords covered so far is set out in Figure 4. There are clearly many more variations of simple time rhythm, but these basics have been found to cover general primary school needs.

Figure 4

160

Try clapping this through from beginning to end, but start at a very steady pace or you will find the 'run-ning fas-ter' goes quicker than you can clap!

Compound rhythms

Compound rhythms sound as if they are more complicated than rhythms described as 'simple'. They are, in fact, as easy to understand, because by using word rhythms there is a feeling of how the rhythm moves which is not complicated by mathematical calculations about relative lengths of notes. There are fewer keywords to remember in compound time than in simple time, and the only reason why simple time was presented first is that more classroom material uses this kind of measure. Let us compare a simple rhythm, the beats of which divide into two, and a compound rhythm whose beats divide into three.

Simple:

Walk   Walk   Run-ning   Walk (repeated)

Compound:

Skip-ping-and skip and (repeated)

Many nursery rhymes are in compound time:

Hickory Dickory Dock – the

Mouse ran up the clock.

Here is one that is in simple time:

Baa Baa Black Sheep,

Have you any wool?

In keywords, this would be:

Walk Walk Walk Walk
Run-ning Run-ning Stand.

Because the main beat of compound time is divisible by three, the basic beat looks like a 'walk' with a dot after it. You will remember that this dot makes the note half as long again. This means that 'walk' which is still used for the basic beat in compound time will be represented by the compound time's version of 'walk' which looks like this:

It is made up of:

and   because of the dot.

Here is a rhythm which shows the division of the main beat into three little pulses. Clap it and 'feel' how it works.

Skip-ping-and walk – , skip-ping-and walk

Here is another rhythm for you to try:

Skip-ping-and skip and (repeated)

When it comes to putting dots after notes to make that rather jerky effect, the keywords used can be these:

Skip-ping-and skip-pi-ty (repeated)

There is only one more keyword which needs to be mentioned and that is the one which lasts as long as two 'walks'. This is, again, sta-nd, although because the beats have to be divisible by three, the stand is written in notation as follows:

This is another nursery rhyme; try to identify it. (The name of the rhyme is given on page 162.)

161

Skip and skip and/ walk ≈ skip and
Skip and skip and/ walk ≈ skip and
Walk skip and / walk skip and
Walk walk / stand.

Time signatures

You can tell whether a piece is in simple or compound time by looking at the 'key signature'. This is indicated by the two numbers at the beginning of the piece which look like a fraction, eg. $\frac{3}{4}$. You will see, however, that, unlike a fraction, there isn't a line between the two numbers and, in fact, they mean something much simpler.

If we return to simple time, you will recall that the large four-beat note (a semibreve) looked like this: o

If we think of it as a ONE note, then the two minims (♩) which fit inside it are TWO notes. The crotchet (simple 'walk' ♩) can fit inside the ONE note four times, so it is a FOUR note and the quaver, two of which make the rhythm 'running', can fit eight times into the time space of the ONE note. They are therefore EIGHT notes.

In a time signature, the top number says, 'We have got...' followed by the number, and the bottom number tells you whether the time values are 'walks' or 'stands' or whatever. If it says $\frac{3}{4}$ then there are three FOUR notes in each in each bar. In $\frac{6}{8}$ time, you will see that the beats are divided into two (because there are 'running' time values). Here is an example:

In compound time, you will see $\frac{6}{8}$ or $\frac{9}{8}$ which means that there are a given number of EIGHT notes in the bar and that this number is divisible by three. Here is an example of a rhythm with a compound time signature.

Upbeats

Sometimes a piece of music begins with one or a small group of notes before the first full bar. It was noted in Chapter 15 that the American National Anthem began on an up-beat because of the necessary word emphasis, but this should not be allowed to confuse one in counting the beats in the bar. The up-beat(s) are what is called an 'anacrusis' and this is not included in the beats of the first full bar.

(The nursery-rhyme rhythms for recognition on pages 160 and 162 were 'Incy Wincy Spider' (page 160) and 'Ring-a-ring of roses' (page 162).

Using keyword cards in the classroom

Keyword values can be taught in the classroom using keyword cards. Some specimen cards are illustrated below:

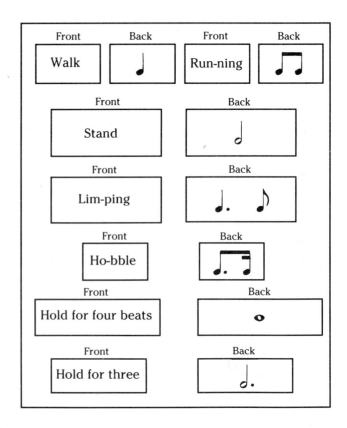

Notice that the cards are of length relative to their time length. This is useful

as children composing rhythmic patterns will see more clearly a mistake in the number of beats in the bar, and will be encouraged to look to see what is wrong. Some specimen compound time cards are illustrated below:

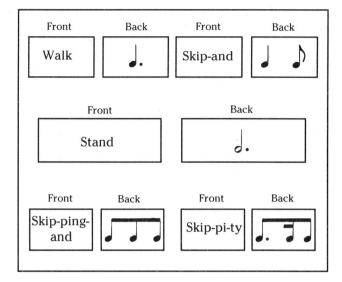

To introduce the idea of keyword cards to the children, face the class and show them a 'walk' card, stating that each time they see the walk symbol, they must say 'walk'. Produce it from behind your back and let the children respond. Having done this two or three times, introduce the 'running' card and go through the same procedure. Now produce one or the other and, once the children can respond correctly, set up a 'sentence' of four cards, music side forwards, on a convenient ledge. These should then be spoken, spoken and clapped and finally clapped by the class. Members of the class can then be invited to come out and 'compose' other rhythms using the two values which can be clapped by the class. Four groups can then be formed and 'walk' and 'running' cards distributed so that each group can compose a four-card (beat) phrase. When this is done, stand centrally and, pointing to one of the groups, count:

1 2 3 4

The group should then play their rhythm. As they finish, and in time for the second indicated group to follow on smoothly without a pause, indicate a second group to play their rhythm. When all have played, continue to point to groups, sometimes singly and sometimes to two at once The clapping should be continuous and successful, providing that the children keep alert and clap their rhythm accurately. Further keyword values can be taught in this way and as time goes on the whole of the 'simple values' will be known.

Either the keywords or the music symbols can be used in group work, according to the needs and abilities of the children. The addition to rhythmic notation of pitch is a simple matter, particularly if the children are given the chance to work it out themselves with pitched percussion instruments or with recorders. Only one thing must be insisted upon, as was emphasised in Chapter 18 (The recorder). Discourage the children from playing from pitched, or staff, notation (that written on five lines) with the names of the notes written underneath the stave. Note names for pitched playing can be written under lines of rhythmic notation, but as soon as the five lines (E, G, B, D and F) are before the children, insist that they use them. There is much published material which encourages children to use notation and the composers are careful to provide parts which contain limited ranges of notes. A number of these have been successfully used by children who learned to read music using 'keywords' and there have been cases in which poor readers of language have succeeded at reading and playing music.

Section 3: Pitch cards

Teaching 'staff notation'

Sets of pitch cards can be made for any range of notes which are thought to be

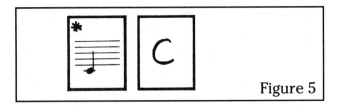

Figure 5

useful in the classroom (Figure 5). The letter name of the note should be written on the back of the card and the asterisk should always be at the top of the card. Page 177 is intended to be helpful in this respect and may be photocopied. The notes have been omitted so that you can make the cards which are appropriate to your own needs. Key signature, time signature and clef cards are also included.

A useful range of notes for which cards can be made is given in Figure 6; note the super and sub-script marks (' or ,) which identify notes which are of the same name but sound at different pitches from the middle octave of notes.

Figure 6

After the copies have been stuck on to card and cut out, the individual notes can be assembled, side by side, by children who are composing a melody.

First, however, the treble clef ( ) must be placed at the beginning. Without this the lines mean nothing; with it the bottom line becomes the E which is found in the middle of the piano keyboard. There are other clefs which make the lines mean different things; the bass clef ( ), which can be seen on piano music, causes the bottom line to become the lowest G that a male singer can reach. The notes of the bass clef rise and meet the notes of the treble clef rather like

two ladders joined together (Figure 7).

A key signature needs to be placed next to the clef and a number of suitable cards are provided for this purpose. The key signatures for some of the scales likely to be useful in the classroom are shown in Figure 8, along with their starting notes. When there is an F# in the key signature, all the F's in the piece are played as F#. Any key signature affects its following notes in this way.

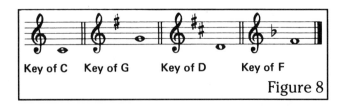

Key of C   Key of G   Key of D   Key of F

Figure 8

The time signature refers to the time values of notes (discussed on page 162) ≈ ONE notes (the long semibreve), the TWO note (the minim), the FOUR note (the crotchet) and the EIGHT note (the quaver). The top number says how many beats there are in the bar, and the bottom number says what their value is. (See Figure 9.)

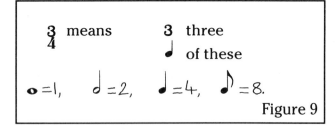

Figure 9

Using pitch cards in the classroom

The practical uses of pitch cards are many and varied but here are a few suggestions.
• If children are composing a melody which

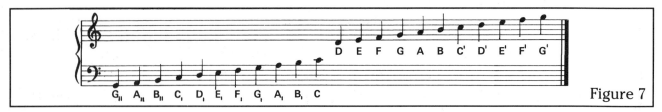

Figure 7

is to be fitted to a chord sequence (see chord cards, page 166) and wish to record what they have composed, the letter-name sides of the cards can be matched to the notes which are stamped upon the glockenspiel or xylophone which is being used. The cards can then be turned over (asterisk at the top) and the notes copied on to manuscript paper. The rhythm of the melody can be recorded by the additional use of keyword cards.

• A set of pitch cards can be made on the back of which in addition to the note name the recorder fingering of the note can be included. This set will have to contain both F and F#, B and B♭ as well as any other sharpened or flattened notes needed since if used with a key signature which requires the sharp or the flat, a different fingering will need to be used. These cards will look like that in Figure 10.

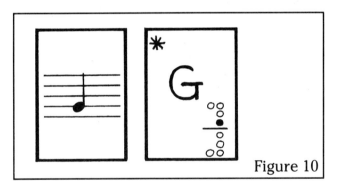

Figure 10

Very often children try to play songs that they have heard on the recorder or some other instrument. Pitch cards, which carry recorder fingerings, will not only help them to put tunes on paper, but they will also encourage the children to seek out and learn notes which may not yet have been dealt with in group recorder sessions. These cards have frequently been used in group recorder sessions in which, as a change from playing from somebody else's music, the children take turns in adding phrases to an 'instant' composition of their own which is then played, changed, played, refined and finally committed to paper. Once children see how the cards work, they usually find new ways of using them.

• A number of pitch cards can be handed

out to groups in composition activities. It may be that the teacher wishes the children to compose but, at the same time, to reinforce an area of pitch-related work covered earlier (for instance, the pentatonic scale). The use of pitch cards to contain the activity seems to work more effectively than the mere statement that such and such notes are to be used. In handling the cards, there is also a continual familiarisation with musical conventions which come more easily in this situation than in a formal lesson.

Section 4: Chord families

In Chapter 15 it was noted that chords are related together in families, and that some members of these chord families appear in a number of key households but function as different kinds of relation. To explain this in terms of human families, consider a father. He is father in his own household but he may be uncle in another while, at the same time, being grandfather in a third.

Some chord families, showing the most active members, are illustrated in this section. In the key of C, the 'parent' chord is that of C (C, E, G) but you will see that it also appears in the key of G where the 'parent' chord is G (G, B, D). Every key – and all twelve musical notes are themselves the 'parent' note of their own key family – contains the same variety of relations. The basic related chords shown on the charts are formed on the first, fourth, fifth and sixth notes of the scale. The three-note chords are called 'triads', and those mentioned above are circled, although all seven 'primary triads' are shown in Figure 11.

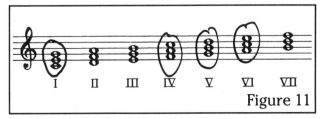

Figure 11

These are the related triads most used in harmony. They can be found in any key, providing you know how many sharps or flats are required in the key signature; a list of these is given at the end of the section.

Each triad, if counted from the note on which it is based, contains the first, third and fifth note. You may notice that one of the family member chords on each grid appears as, for instance, G7. The '7' refers to the seventh note which has been added to make the chord sound better. When the seventh note is added, the fifth note is left out. The basic chord families of four major keys are shown in Figure 12.

Major and minor chords

In the first chart, that of the key of C, there is a chord marked as Am. This means A minor, which differs from the chord of A major in that one note is altered.

A major chord – A, C#, E
A minor chord – A, C, E
D major chord – D, F#, A
D minor chord – D, F, A

The difference in sound is often thought to be that while the major chord is bright and cheerful, the minor chord sounds sad. Play the two chords and see what you think. It would certainly not be good to teach children that this 'bright' and 'sad' distinction is any sort of fact. It is far better that children come to their own conclusions about how the difference in sound is to be described. Children should be allowed to 'play' with harmonic progressions and re-organisations of chords. They will then recognise for themselves how their own cultural system of music works; to have to be told, as were children of the last generation, is unproductive and a very great bore!

A system which enables children to try out harmonic combinations by the use of coloured blocks called 'The Colour Chord Blocks' is at present being developed by the Enterprise Unit at The University of Central England in Birmingham. In this system the triad on chord I (see Figure 11 on page 165) is represented by a red block, while triads II, III, IV, V and VI are represented by light blue, yellow, dark

Chord family of C: C, D, E, F, G, A, B					
G	C	B	E	B	A
E	A	G	C	G	F
C	F	F	A	E	D
C	F	G7	Am	Em	Dm

Chord family of D: D, E, F#, G, A, B, C#					
A	D	C#	F#	C#	B
F#	B	A	D	A	G
D	G	G	B	F#	E
D	G	A7	Bm	F#	Em

Chord family of G: G, A, B, C, D, E, F#					
D	G	F#	B	F#	E
B	E	D	G	D	C
G	C	C	E	B	A
G	C	D7	Em	Bm	Am

Chord family of F: F, G, A, B♭, C, D, E					
C	F	E	A	E	D
A	D	C	F	C	B♭
F	B♭	B♭	D	A	G
F	B♭	C7	Dm	Am	Gm

Figure 12

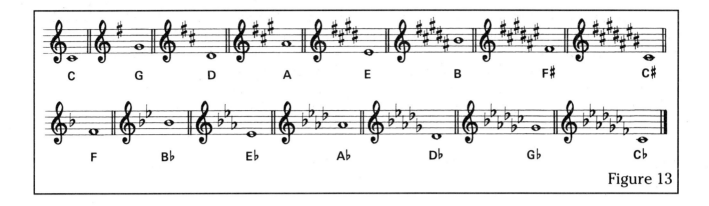

Figure 13

blue, green and pink blocks respectively. This enables children to discuss harmonically related chords in 'user-friendly' terms. For example, a Y6 girl said, when organising an harmonic accompaniment, 'You've got to start and finish on red.' This, according to our Western tradition, is true, but in most harmony text books it takes several pages to explain. She had been given a means of expressing this truth in terms which she understood from her practical experience. The harmonic rule had been allowed to dawn naturally instead of being stated as fact.

Major scale key signatures

The major scale key signatures are shown in Figure 13.

Section 5: Specimen chord sequences

A variety of chord sequences can be given to children who, having played and listened to them, can then add melodies. Specimen chord sequences are given on page 178. Some are short sequences which can be played as ostinati and others are accompaniments of existing tunes. This does not mean that that particular tune has to be found, but it does mean that the invented tune will have the same pattern of harmonies and could be played with the original. This common harmonic pattern occurs in many songs. Let half your class sing one of the songs mentioned below and the other half the other at the same time!

Group 1 Bobby Shaftoe
Group 2 Skip to my Lou

Add a further group to these and they can sing 'Michael Finnegan' at the same time as the other two groups sing their songs.

The specimen chord sequences given on page 178 have been re-arranged so that each player uses the minimum number of notes, and no notes are played by more than one player. The name of the chord is given in the shaded boxes. The way in which this re-arrangement can be made is described in Chapter 15.

Section 6: Rhythm grids and word rhythm compositions

When children have learned to listen carefully to a rhythm and are able to repeat it accurately, it is time to encourage them to play from some kind of notation. The reason for this is two-fold. Work on existing pieces which were provided by the teacher and played days before can continue without having to start again from scratch, and there will be a means by which children can record their own pieces so that the essential developmental process in composition can take place. It also provides them with the opportunity to play extended rhythms which would be too unwieldy to commit to memory.

Rhythm grids provide an excellent means of recording simple compositions and have the added benefit of producing a recognisable feeling of equal sections or phrases within the piece. No teacher need worry that they themselves cannot compose a rhythm-grid piece for use by their class. Once a grid is drawn, a useful piece of material can easily be produced. A simple example is given Figure 14.

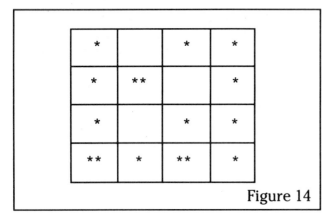

Figure 14

This kind of grid can be played by clapping, tapping or with the use of an instrument and the teacher can indicate, with a pointer, the route to be taken. The conventional 'top line, left to right, followed by the second line and so on' route may serve well for a start, and to complement the scanning direction used in reading, but infinite variety can be introduced by following different paths. The grid can also be played in canon, one line for each section but, as can be seen in Figure 15, different sounds can be notated.

The next example, shown in Figure 16, is entitled 'Bicycle Music'. It is the kind of composition which infants can both play and compose. You will see that the first line has a different emphasis from the rest.

Ped-al	Ped-al	Ped-al
Bi-cy-cle		Bell
Han-dle		Bars
I've got a		sad-dle bag

Figure 16

Practise each line singly with your class and then try putting any of lines two, three and four together. Let the children say the rhythms first before saying and clapping. Only then should they try it by clapping alone. When this is secure, introduce the complexity of the first line with its cross rhythm. It would be better to omit the first line if the children are not sufficiently experienced to sustain the cross rhythm. When, however, they are able to put the two rhythms together they will, as many children have done before, find the effect of the cross rhythms great fun. The 'handle bars' line can be spoken in two ways, as is illustrated below, but the teacher must decide for herself whether this approach is advisable.

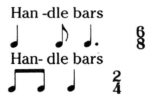

#	**	#	#	You can choose sounds for each symbol, ie.
/	$	**	/	# finger click * clap / stamp
**	#	$	$	$ cheek pop (finger in side of mouth)
/ #	**	**	#	Groups can play their own sound, or all can play all symbols. Can be played as a round or as four separate parts.

Figure 15

The last example of a word-rhythm composition is called 'Tiger, Tiger'. The letters of the word 'tiger' have been arranged so that a most exciting effect is possible with fairly experienced children (Figure 17).

T	I	G	T	I	G	E	R	E	R
T		G	T		G		R		R
T	I		T	I		E		E	
		G			G	E	R	E	R
T	I	G	T	I	G	E	R	E	R

GRRRRRRRRRRRRR!

Figure 17

What is on the grid is not played through as if one were playing a Beethoven symphony. Repeat lines when you wish, start playing where you please and treat the whole thing as a resource from which a new piece can be made. Make sure, by clear instructions or expressive conducting, that the children know when to end or the 'Grrrrrrrrrrrrr...' will be less effective – 'and that,' as one lad remarked, 'is the best bit!'

Section 7: Music at storytime

Each of the three stories which follow was made up as the need arose. One encourages the handling of instruments and the possibilities of using them to express ideas, feelings and sound; one was invented specifically to teach the musical concept of 'high' and 'low' sounds; the third brings together music and mathematics in an attempt to help children tell the time.

The stories are presented here mainly to show how teachers can adapt existing stories or make up their own to suit the needs of their class.

A giant came

This story invites children to improvise sounds rather than music. This is the beginning of composition with the awareness that instruments can be manipulated to produce required effects. There is repetition in the story which encourages the composition of musical sections to which the players will become accustomed. This device enables everyone to take part.

Once upon a time there was a great forest of trees. The trees were very happy. No one bothered them. The sun shone through their leaves, the birds sang in their branches and the bees buzzed from flower to flower.

Discuss with the children how they can represent the noises, appearance and mood of the forest through sound. How can they represent sunlight through the branches? What about bird song and the bees? How can they make a happy and perhaps lazy sound? Adopt this approach throughout the story where appropriate.

But one day, among all these pleasant sounds a new sound was heard in the forest. It was the sound of a giant who had come to live in the forest. He had tired of living in his cave on the top of a mountain. It had been cold and windy and wet, so he had decided to build a house in the shelter of the forest. The trees heard his huge footsteps coming nearer and nearer.

The trees saw that over his shoulder was a great silver axe. They had never seen an axe before, but they quickly learned what it was for. The giant took it from his shoulder and soon the chopping sound of it cutting into one of the trees rang throughout the forest.

The tree began to rock and to shiver and then it crashed to the ground.

The giant picked up the tree by the trunk and dragged it away.

'If the giant is building a house,' said a squirrel, 'he will want a lot of wood. He is a very big giant.'

The trees swayed together and murmured in their soft tree voices. 'If he is

169

building a house,' they said, 'he will cut down more trees.'

The next day the trees woke up as usual at sunrise. The birds began to sing and the squirrels began to run about in the branches. As it grew warmer, the bees buzzed out from their holes in the hollow trees and all the usual sounds of the forest could be heard.

But then everyone stopped and listened because, in the distance, the sound of the giant's footsteps began to echo through the forest. It came nearer and nearer and nearer and then there was the sound once again of his axe cutting the tree.

The tree began to rock and to shiver and then it crashed to the ground.

The giant picked up the tree by the trunk and dragged it away.

This was terrible. The trees swayed together, filling the air with their murmuring. 'What will happen? Perhaps he will cut the whole forest down.'

The squirrels, who made their dreys in the branches, were worried. 'We shall have nowhere to live,' they chattered.

The bees who lived in the hollow trees flew this way and that with an angry buzzing.

'We must do something about this,' they said.

The next day, because they had always done it, the birds began to sing as the sun rose and all the other pleasant summer sounds began to fill the forest.

Then everyone stopped and listened. In the distance the sound of the giant's footsteps could be heard, coming nearer and nearer and nearer. But then there was another sound. At first it was like one of the forest sounds but it grew louder and louder and louder. It grew louder as the sound of the giant's footsteps came nearer. Finally it was so loud that even the giant stopped and listened.

It was the sound of all the bees. They buzzed angrily as they set out towards the giant. The giant had just taken his axe from his shoulder but now the furious swarm of bees rushed towards him like a black cloud.

At first he waved his axe at them over his head. Then he began to dance and to flap at the air with his hands. Then he ran... and ran... and ran. And he was never seen again.

The bees returned to their nests and the trees swayed together murmuring. 'I believe he's gone. Do you think he's gone?'

The forest began to fill with its usual pleasant summer sounds and the squirrels, once again, began to run about in the branches. The sun smiled.

The mouse story

This story is useful with young children to establish conventional pitch vocabulary relating to high and low notes. Similar stories which include a classroom game/activity can also be made up. Three chime bars are required to play the game: one low, one high and one between the two. A cardboard or construction-kit model of the church tower with three windows, one above the other, would also be useful.

There was once an old church in the village of Appletree Green. The three windows in the tall tower looked out over the village and when the bells rang to tell the time, the people said, 'Time for school', or 'Time for lunch', or 'Time to go to bed', or just set their clocks, because in all the years that the clock had been telling them the time, it had never been wrong.

In the tower where the three great bells hung there lived several families of mice. There were mothers and fathers, brothers and sisters, aunties and uncles, as well as grandmas and grandads, and even a few great-grandmas and great-grandads.

But down in the village there were even more mice and, when a mouse in the clock tower had a birthday, there would most likely be a little present left where it could be found, and then the birthday mouse would have to write a thank-you letter.

'Dear Auntie and Uncle Greywhiskers,

Thank you very much for my nice woolly hat. It will keep my ears warm. It was very kind of you.

Love from White Toes.'

The mother and father mice were very careful to see that the thank-you letters were written the day after the birthday and that the writing was very neat.

Some of the mice lived a long way from the church and the letters had to be sent by post but this was not difficult as the Post Office was just opposite the church door. The mice ran down the bell ropes, jumped to the floor and ran through a little secret door which was never locked across to the Post Office.

Mr Grump looked after the church and cut the grass in the churchyard. One day when it was raining he unlocked the old church door and went inside, carefully wiping his feet. He looked at the carpet below the bell ropes.

'Oh dear,' he said. Across the floor were several little muddy footmarks.

'We've got mice,' said Mr Grump. 'We'll have to get rid of them. Dirty footmarks in my nice clean bell tower. That won't do! That won't do at all!'

He set off to the nearby farm muttering, 'Mice in my nice clean church... Won't do at all. Not at all!'

A little while later he was back. Under his arm there was a huge ginger tom cat. 'Now, Algernon,' said Mr Grump. 'You're going to live here and I shall bring you milk and some food every day. But there are mice in this church and it won't do. You can eat all you catch and I don't want any more dirty footmarks on the floor. Make sure you wipe your feet, too,' he added.

Algernon licked his lips. He had had to share the mice with the other cats at the farm. Now he had mice all of his own.

Twinkletail Mouse was just finishing a letter. Her mother looked at it to see if it was neatly written and said, 'Very nice, dear. Now I'll put it in an envelope and you can take it to the Post Office.'

Twinkletail began to run down the bell rope but then she stopped and sniffed.

'Mum,' she called, 'Mum! There's something down below. I don't like the smell of it.'

Father Mouse ran down the rope and then came back looking worried.

'Cat,' he said. 'There's a cat down below, and he's got a saucer of milk. I think he's come to stay.'

That night the mice had a meeting.

'If there's a cat living down there, we shan't be able to post our letters,' said Head Mouse.

'What we want is a postman who can fly down to the Post Office. We'll all go to bed now and tomorrow we'll get one.'

The next morning the mice all met together on one of the window ledges. Head Mouse went to the edge and called to a little bird with a blue cap.

'Here, Bluecap,' he called. 'Come here a minute, will you?'

The bird flew down and was rather surprised to see all the mice. Head Mouse went up to him.

'How would you like to be a postman?' asked Head Mouse.

'Me?' said the bird.

'Yes,' said Head Mouse. 'We want you to be our postman.'

'Do I get to drive a red van?' asked the bird.

'I'm afraid not,' said Head Mouse. 'We want you to be a flying postman.'

The bird thought for a bit.

'All right,' he said. 'What do I have to do?'

'You come in here when we call you and take our letters down to the Post Office,' said Head Mouse.

'How do I know which window?' asked the bird.

'Oh, just come in any window and fly down to where we are,' said Head Mouse.

'In there?' said the bird, looking nervously inside the tower.

'Yes,' said Head Mouse.

'I'm not going in there,' said the bird.

'Why not?' said Head Mouse.

'There are owls in there,' said the bird.

Head Mouse looked a bit cross. 'There aren't any owls in here,' he said. 'Do you think we'd live here if there were owls?'

'I don't care,' said the bird. 'I'm not going in there.'

Then Twinkletail had a brilliant idea. 'If we wanted him to come to the highest window, we could tap on the highest bell. Tap on the highest bell, Whitespot.'

Sound the highest pitched chime bar.

'If we wanted him to come to the lowest window, we could tap the lowest bell. Tap on the lowest bell, Flopear.'

Sound the lowest pitched chime bar.

'And if we wanted him to come to the middle window,' said Head Mouse, 'we ring the bell which sounds the middle sound. You are a very clever mouse. You will probably be Head Mouse one day.'

'Let's have that again,' said the bird.

At this point, ask whether, after sounding all three bells, the high, the low or the middle bell is sounded. The chime bars can be hidden and the children can take turns in being the mouse calling the Postbird so that the others can say whether he should go to the high, low or middle windows, or whether it is the high, low or middle bell. Questions such as, 'Is the middle window higher or lower than the lowest window?' can be asked and eventually, 'Which sound is higher or lower than another?'

The bird soon got very good at finding the right window, though he never came into the tower.

Algernon became rather lazy and spent a lot of time sitting in the sun.

'You're a good cat,' said Mr Grump. 'No sign of a mouse since you came. Have a nice saucer of milk. Here's some cat food – your favourite.'

The bat who needed to tell the time

This is a story which uses the chimes of a clock to help teach telling the time. You will need three chime bars: G, E and C. The hours are played by the C bar and the 'ting tang' which sounds for each quarter is played by the G and E bars. You will also need some kind of large clock face.

Flitimus Bat was hanging by his feet from a rusty nail in the bell tower of a church in the country. Something gave him a terrific nip on the tummy and he let go with one foot and scratched; a big fat flea dived for cover in his fur.

Flitimus didn't mind the fleas. He had always had them, but they were a nuisance when they woke him up in the middle of the day when all sensible bats were asleep.

Flitimus lived with several other bats, and when the sun went down and the nice soft darkness turned the trees to a blue blur for all those who came out in the day, Flitimus and his friends would leave the tower and fly squeaking among the juicy insects that filled the air. Moth was his favourite and at this time of the year there were plenty to be had.

Flitimus sighed. 'I wonder how long it is to breakfast?' he thought.

Something was scratching about on the window ledge. Flitimus twisted his ankles so that his whole body turned towards the sunlit window. The light made him blink.

A sparrow was hopping about on the ledge, pecking at a piece of bread and nervously looking this way and that to be ready for any danger. He saw Flitimus blinking at him from the inside of the tower.

'What you are doing hanging head downwards, O mouse?' asked the sparrow.

Flitimus gave his wings an irritated flutter. 'I am not a mouse, O feathery wedge-face,' he said.

'You can call me Spad,' said the sparrow.

'I am Flitimus Bat,' said Flitimus with dignity. 'And I am supposed to be asleep.'

'What do you want to sleep for on a nice day like this?' said Spad, cleaning his beak on the window ledge. 'All sorts of things are going on out here today. I just gave a dragonfly a peck; it crashed into the pond and something swooped up and swallowed it.'

Flitimus was interested. 'That's not a fly I know,' he said. 'Do they taste nice?'

'I've never really eaten one,' said Spad. 'They're longer than me but you know how it is. Something moves so you peck at it. If it looks dangerous, you leave it alone. If you like it, you eat it.'

'And this one fell into the pond,' said Flitimus. 'So you couldn't.'

'Easy come, easy go,' said Spad.

'I often fly over to the pond at dusk,' said Flitimus. 'I can't see in the day. I crash into things and it makes my head ache. I was disturbed once by a human who came up here and I flew out by accident. I couldn't find my way back so I had to wait for night.'

Spad shivered and fluffed up his feathers. 'I got chased off my night perch once,' he said. 'Spent the night on the ground under a bush.'

He looked so uneasy that Flitimus changed the subject.

'I really must be getting back to sleep,' he said. 'Only I wish I knew how long it is to dusk – I'm getting hungry.'

At that moment there was a rumble and a clanking sound from inside the works of the clock and the two smaller bells went, 'Ting tang, ting tang, ting tang.'

'There you are,' said Spad. 'Quarter to.'

'Quarter to what?' asked Flitimus.

'Don't know,' said Spad. 'But it is certainly a quarter to something.'

Flitimus scratched thoughtfully. 'I have often wondered what all that clanking was,' he said.

Spad hopped inside the window. 'Don't you know what it means?'

'No, not really,' confessed Flitimus.

'Well, you can tell the time from it,' said Spad. 'If it goes ting tang, it's a quarter past.'

'Quarter past what?' asked Flitimus.

'Quarter past what it said last,' offered Spad. 'When it goes ting tang, ting tang, ting tang, ting tang – DONG – it's one o'clock. Then when it goes ting tang after that, it means it's a quarter past one and when it goes ting tang, ting tang after that it's half past one....'

'And when it goes ting tang, ting tang, ting tang after that it's three quarters past one?' said Flitimus.

'That's the same as a quarter to two,' said Spad.

Flitimus scratched again. 'How did you learn all this?' he asked.

'Been to school,' said Spad proudly. 'I go down there at half past ten in the morning to get the crisp crumbs. I sit on the window ledge and the children put their crumbs out. Before I could tell the time, I was sometimes early and the children were learning it. The teacher had some ting tang things and a DONG thing and they had to move the hands on a clock.'

'What's the time now?' asked Flitimus.

'It's nearly ting tang, ting tang, ting tang, ting tang, DONG, DONG, DONG, DONG, DONG, DONG,' said Spad.

'That sounds a very long time to breakfast,' said Flitimus with a groan.

As if the clock had been waiting for Flitimus to finish, the rumble and clanking sounded from inside and the four quarters sounded. Ting tang, ting tang, ting tang, ting tang. There was a pause, then more clanking and rumbling. 'DONG,' said the clock six times.

'Six o'clock,' said Flitimus. 'That is a long time to breakfast.'

'Six o'clock,' said 'Orrid 'Orace.

His name was really Horace and he really was horrid, but that was the way he spoke as well as the way he behaved. He made his living by catching rabbits and selling their fur, and trapping moles and stealing the eggs from birds' nests. He also made snares and traps for pheasants and once he had sold a baby fox cub to a pet shop.

His friend was called 'Enry. 'Enry wasn't so bad, but he was silly and did whatever the people he was with did. When he was cutting the grass round the church and talked to the vicar, he was quite nice, but when he was with Horace he could be horrid.

'Six o'clock,' said Horrid Horace again. 'Where's he got to?'

A figure like a worn-out scarecrow was coming along the church path.

'Where you been?' said Horace, not making it sound like a question.

'I lost the sack,' said Henry. 'I stopped to find it but I lost it.'

'We don't want no sack *yet*,' said Horace. 'I told you. We want to see the Vicar. *Tomorrow* night we want the sack. We don't want no sack *tonight*.'

'Sorry,' said Henry.

'Tomorrow night,' said Horace, 'we're going to get the bats.'

''Orace,' said Henry.

'What?' said Horace.

'What do we want bats for?'

'*We* don't want bats,' said Horace. '*We* don't want no bats, but there's this gent who does. He wants bats – not *us*. He's going to *pay* us for the bats.'

'Oh,' said Henry.

Horace peered towards the vicarage.

''Orace,' said Henry.

'What now?'

'What does this gent want the bats for?'

Horace sighed. '*He* don't want bats,' he said. '*He* don't want no bats. His snakes wants bats. Keeps a lot of bat-eating snakes, he does. Dead bats is no good. Live bats they likes. Mice and sparrows they likes – alive. But they likes live bats best.'

The Vicar was coming along the path.

'I'm sorry I'm late,' said the vicar. 'The ladies who do the flowers in the church came to see me just as I was coming out.'

'That's all right,' said Horace. 'Must 'ave the pretty flowers right.'

'Indeed!' said the Vicar. 'I see you've got some old clothes on. Just the thing if you want to go up the tower.'

Henry was going to say that this was what he usually wore, but Horace trod on his toe and gave him a look that made him decide to say nothing.

'We shan't be long,' said Horace. 'We only want to 'ave a quick look. 'Enry here an' me went up when we was boys and he's always saying as how he would like to go up again, don't you, 'Enry?'

Henry was going to say something, but Horace trod on his toe and gave him another look that made him decide to say nothing.

They reached the door and the vicar gave Horace the key to the tower. 'I'll be in the vestry when you've finished,' he said.

'We'll only be ten minutes,' said Horace.

'No hurry, no hurry,' said the vicar.

The steps to the bell chamber went round and round and up and up and Henry

175

began to feel sick. Just as he thought he was going to be sick, they came into the space at the top of the tower. There was a wooden walkway round the outside and the three bells hung in a big frame made from huge pieces of wood.

'I can't see no bats,' said Henry.

'That's why we can't just walk in and catch them,' said Horace. 'We've got to set nets before they go out and collect the nets when they're all caught. They're all in here in the daytime but they go out at nine o'clock. I seen 'em.'

'There's one hanging on that rusty nail up there,' said Henry. 'Up there, look!'

''Orrible, ain't they?' said Horace. 'Look at 'im! Ain't he ugly?'

Flitimus, who had just woken up again, gave a twitch of rage.

Horace took the big iron key from his pocket and also a large flat tin. He opened the tin which was full of soap, smoothed down so that the surface was as level as glass.

'Warmed it up,' said Horace. 'It melts.' He pressed the key into the soap and when he took it out again, the exact shape of the key was left behind. 'That's what we need,' he said.

'What for?' asked Henry.

'So that we can make another key, stupid,' said Horace. 'Why do you think we came up here? To look at the view?'

Henry went to the window and looked at the view. Then he looked down at the ground and came back to Horace in a hurry. 'No,' he said. 'I don't want to look at the view. I don't like the view.'

'Right, then,' said Horace. 'Down we go, and make sure you tell the vicar that it took you back to when you was a boy.'

'What for?' said Henry.

'Just say it,' growled Horace.

Flitimus had just got back to sleep after being disturbed by the two humans when he felt a terrific nip on his tummy. He let go with one foot and scratched but there was no flea. He opened his eyes to see Spad perching on his rusty nail.

'Wake up!' shouted Spad. 'Wake up!'

'Is it breakfast time?' asked Flitimus hopefully.

'No,' said Spad firmly. 'It is not. You and the other bats are in terrible danger. You must do what I say and get it right or you will be eaten by snakes.'

He told Flitimus what one of his friends had heard at the gate of the churchyard. 'You get up at nine o'clock, don't you?'

'Do we?' asked Flitimus.

'Yes,' said Spad. 'Now, what do the bells do at nine?'

'ting tang, ting tang, ting tang, ting tang, DONG, DONG, DONG, DONG, DONG, DONG, DONG DONG... er...'

'DONG,' said Spad.

'Yes,' said Flitimus.

'Well, you've got to get up at quarter past eight.'

'That's ting tang after it's gone DONG, DONG, DONG, DONG, DONG, DONG, DONG, DONG?' said Flitimus.

'Right,' said Spad. 'Now, fly out at quarter past eight and sit on the top of the tower until breakfast time.'

'Tonight?' asked Flitimus.

Spad jumped up and down with rage.

'No,' he shouted. 'Tomorrow night, or you are snake dinner.'

At midnight the next night, two shadowy figures slipped through the door at the bottom of the tower and began to climb the stairs to collect the nets which they had put up earlier. Henry left the door open.

The vicar, who couldn't sleep and had gone to get a book from the vestry, found the door ajar.

'Funny,' he thought. 'Those men must have left the door open.'

The vicar locked the door. There was only a keyhole on the outside.

'Not one bloomin' bat,' said Horace. 'Not one bloomin' bat.'

'Door's stuck,' said Horace. He kicked it. The door didn't mind. It was two hundred years old and five centimetres thick. It didn't even rattle.

'It's dark in here,' wailed Henry.

Flitimus sat on the top of the tower eating a fat moth. He chuckled.

Pitch cards for staff notation, page 163

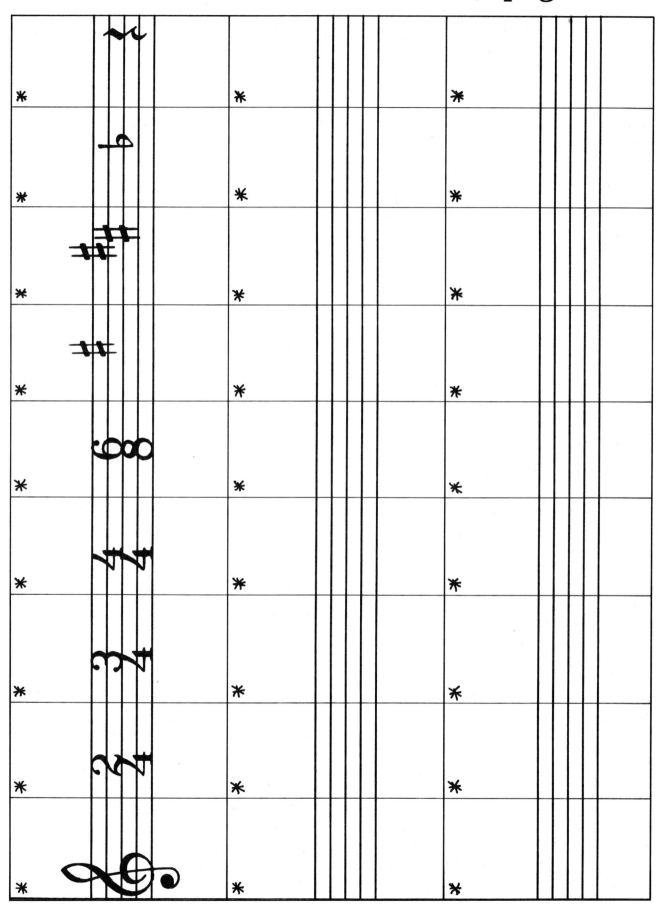

Specimen chord sequences, page 167

Key of D: D, E, F#, G, A, B, C#, D

Player	D	D	D	D	A7	A7	D	D
1	A	A	A	A	A	A	A	A
2	F#	F#	F#	F#	G	G	F#	F#
3	D	D	D	D	C#	C#	D	D

Key of G: G, A, B, C, D, E, F#, G

G	C	Em	D7	C	D7	G	G
D	E	E	D	E	D	D	D
B	C	B	C	C	C	B	B
G	G	G	F#	G	F#	G	G

Key of G: G, A, B, C, D, E, F#, G

G	G	Em	Em	C	D7	G	G
D	D	E	E	E	D	D	D
B	B	B	B	C	C	B	B
G	G	G	G	G	F#	G	G

Key of G: G, A, B, C, D, E, F#, G

G	G	D7	D7	G	G	D7	G
D	D	D	D	D	D	D	D
B	B	C	C	B	B	C	B
G	G	F#	F#	G	G	F#	G

Key of C: C, D, E, F, G, A, B, C

C	C	Am	Am	Dm	G7	F	C
G	G	A	A	A	G	A	G
E	E	E	E	F	F	F	E
C	C	C	C	D	B	C	C

Key of F: F, G, A, B♭, C, D, E, F

F	C7	F	F
C	C	C	C
A	B♭	A	A
F	E	F	F

Key of C: C, D, E, F, G, A, B, C

C	C	C	C	F	G7	C	C
G	G	G	G	A	G	G	G
E	E	E	E	F	F	E	E
C	C	C	C	C	B	C	C

Key of D: D, E, F#, G, A, B, C#, D

D	Em	A7	D
A	B	A	A
F#	G	G	F#
D	E	C#	D

Resources

This section contains information which relates to musical publications appropriate to the primary age range, and some attempt has been made to indicate the stage of school life at which they might be used.

General

A & C Black publish an excellent selection of primary music books, and these are listed in their catalogue entitled *Books for Children, Books for Schools*. A thematic *Index to 26 A and C Black Songbooks* is also available from A & C Black, Trade Department and this is also most useful for the teacher who is looking for songs on specific themes – for example, parts of the body, the sea, separation, etc. Many of these books are already widely known and include *Apusskidu: 56 Songs for Children, Okki-tokki-unga; 55 Action Songs for Children*, and many others in that successful series. The style and format of most of these books will require some ability to play the piano and to be able to organise the playing of parts for classroom instruments.

Schott & Co have produced a most interesting series of teaching books called *Beaters* which encourage the use of classroom instruments. They cover all aspects of the primary curriculum – physical skills, listening skills, performing and composing.

Although it is suggested that any instruments can be employed, it is clear that good quality instruments are required and that a comprehensive set will be needed by a school contemplating the use of these books. The order in which the instruments need to be bought, when embarking upon the use of these books, is clearly stated, and this ensures that such instruments are well and purposefully used. Some familiarity with the work of Carl Orff (*Schulwerk*) is required in the use of this series, though one can learn a good deal from the included material. An ability to read simple notation is sometimes required and it is also necessary to have an understanding of pitched notation in treble and bass clefs.

Once time is taken to study this material, a world of rich possibilities is opened up, and teachers with some musical knowledge should have no difficulty in employing this material.

The good thing about this material is that it is not a consecutive scheme, and teachers can choose the book or books which suit them and the needs of their children. Also non-specialist teachers will find approachable books among the titles, though the help of a school music co-ordinator or adviser might be an advantage in setting up stimulating and enjoyable work.

Music in the early years

Oxford Primary Music (Stage 1) Jean Gilbert and Leonora Davies (1986), OUP. There is an excellent collection of ideas in the teacher's book for Reception and Y1. The use of familiar sounds, sound stories, games, action songs and sound-making activities are all covered and presented in useable forms. Work cards are contained in the teacher's pack and the song book contains plenty of songs at a pitch which is eminently suitable for beginner voices. Ability to play the guitar is an advantage but not essential. A tape contains much useful material, including environmental sounds and songs, from the song book. This is altogether a valuable pack and will be a boon to the general class teacher.

Oxford Primary Music (Stage 2) Jean Gilbert and Leonora Davies (1989), OUP. This pack resembles Stage 1 but provides material suitable for use in Y1 – Y3. The publishers suggest that this is purely infant school material, but the spread of ability in schools and the attractiveness of the songs in the song book tempt one to think that this pack could well be of use in the first year of the junior school.

High low dolly pepper Veronica Clark (1991), A & C Black.
This is a resource book of poems, songs, activities and games with which an infant teacher can explore music with her class. There can be few books with so many valuable and relevant suggestions and activities to the page.

Adventures in Music for the Very Young Gillian Wakely (1984), Schott & Co.
This book contains singing games for Reception to Y1 children, but also deals with the somewhat specialist concept of music reading readiness at a very young age. The improvement of singing and playing is covered and a list of music for guided listening is included. This book would be of interest to the general reception teacher, though help from the music co-ordinator might be required in the use of notated songs.

Up, up and Away Derek Pearson (1987), OUP.
This book is principally intended for use in special education but would be useful in the early years. It is a resource book containing songs, poems, games and activities which would surely have value in a wider area than that suggested by the writer. Guitar music appears in chord form which is written out in notation and this may seem forbidding to many who would otherwise enjoy using this book. It would be a pity if only guitar players were to use it because, apart from the chime bar and rhythmic work included, it contains so many short, effective fun songs which are never banal, nor silly, nor patronising. OUP also publishes books for handicapped and autistic children, and these and many other early years music books are listed at the back of this book.

Strike Five Peter Sideway (1984), Schott & Co.
This book, suitable for use with Y1 – Y6, discusses the choice, playing technique and care of instruments and the introduction of pitched playing when sufficient rhythmic skills are attained. The use of the pentatonic scale and simple accompaniments to songs are described in an approachable way, designed to help the general class teacher.

Music in Action Michael Lane (1984), Schott & Co.
This book is suitable for use with Y1 – Y7 children. It includes ideas on improvisation, word rhythms, playing skills, music with stories and activities emphasising the expressive quality of music. There are interesting sections on the use of the voice and ideas for music-related projects. A really valuable book which poses no problems for the non-specialist.

Dr Knickerbocker Diana Thompson and Shirley Winfield (1984), Schott & Co.
This book can be used with Reception to Y6 children. It builds up a feeling for pulse and rhythmic playing skill and contains eminently playable music games, providing many excellent opportunities for exploring sound and the capabilities of instruments. Composition relating to poems and dramatic situations is encouraged and the handling and making of instruments realistically discussed.

Scholastic Collections: Songs Peter Morrell (1992), Scholastic Publications Ltd.
A lively collection of songs for the whole primary range. Organised thematically with simple piano accompaniments and guitar chords.

Middle primary to Y7

Catch a Round Peter Sideway (1984), Schott & Co.
This book contains everything you need to know about using rounds. It includes 30 new rounds with approachable accompaniments. This book is not only valuable to children but would be informative and useful to the less musically practised teacher. This book also encourages an approach to creativity.

A Swag of Songs: 46 Australian Songs, Old and New June Epstein (Ed.) (1984), A & C Black.
An excellent collection of Australian songs, old and new. There are a few Aboriginal songs which are accompanied with simple instruments, but most of the 46 songs require a competent pianist.

Phantasmagoria: 33 Songs, Story Lines and Sound Adventures Kaye Umansky (1988), A & C Black.
A song and ideas book full of delightful junior school humour. It contains songs, playlets and stories with piano accompaniments of a fairly easy standard, and invites the inclusion of pitched and unpitched instruments in an uncomplicated way. Great fun for all except the terminally 'grown-up'.

The Singing Sack: 28 Song-stories from Around the World (1989), A & C Black.
Compiled at the National Folktale Centre, this book offers unaccompanied songs. A cassette can be obtained to help the teachers who may need help with musical notation. This is an enchanting collection, though many of the songs have to be sung in foreign languages which are written phonetically. Many, however, are not, and the stories themselves make this a splendid resource book.

Sing a Story: Songs about Children's Favourite Stories Graham Westcott (1989), A & C Black.
This is a book of songs which relate to well-known stories with accompaniments for guitar or simple standard piano. The bibliography at the end gives details of the books referred to which are junior age range reading.

Game-songs with Prof. Dogg's Troupe: 44 Songs and Games with Activities Harriet Powell (1983), A & C Black.
A book of collected songs with activities and helpful instructions on how to use it. There are simple piano accompaniments, chords for guitars and a tape to help teachers who do not play an instrument. Most valuable for use with Y2 – Y4 children.

Sounds Around Cliff Matthews (1991), Longman.
Two excellent books which lead children in the class of the non-specialist teacher to an understanding of the basic elements of musical notation. There are parts for recorder, guitar, voices and percussion and the work is carefully structured in a useful and logical progression. Both class activities and group work are catered for.

Let's Make Music (Novello Music Projects).
This resource pack can be used with 9–14 year olds and comes with a book of work cards and a video tape which demonstrates how sounds from the environment and sounds produced by everyday sources (radiators, waste paper etc) can be turned into useful sounds for composition. The compositions illustrated on the video may seem a little forbidding to those unaccustomed to this kind of work, and 'Norman', who demonstrates on the video, does introduce his ideas at lightning speed, but the material is an interesting introduction to graphic scores and the use of sounds around us.

Festivals Jean Gilbert (1987), OUP.
This must be one of the finest multicultural song books ever produced. Useful in both infant and junior schools, it contains a mass of cross-curricular interest and opportunities for children to improvise and play accompaniments. Easy piano accompaniments are provided for some of the songs, and guitar chords in comfortable keys provide another useful alternative. With this book it is possible to learn about those religious festivals which are important to specific groups of children in school and to enable them to share them with children of other faiths.

Zmm! Zmm! 50 Songs from Schools Broadcasts Douglas Coombes (1987), OUP.

This song book contains chord symbols, melodic accompaniments and parts for unpitched percussion. It will be useful for the teacher who can read music, or someone with access to assistance in learning the melodies. A tape would have been useful, but is probably impracticable with so large a collection of songs.

Trig Trog Douglas Coombes (1987), OUP. This is a companion volume to *Zmm! Zmm!*

The Oxford Assembly Book June Tillman (1989), OUP.
This provides a wealth of ideas suitable for Y2 – Y7 assemblies which are grouped and cross-referenced most usefully. Piano parts require reasonable skill and, although some classroom instrumental parts are very simple, others have to be read from music and would need to be written out for the purpose. Others can be sung unaccompanied, or in unison with a melodic instrument, so this is a small matter. As a resource book, it is highly successful and the help of the school music co-ordinator should enable all the songs to be used, despite the occasional key signatures which may test the players to the limit.

Shoo Fly Francine Watson Coleman and Margaret Murray (1984), Schott & Co.
For use with Y3 – Y6 children, this book is a 'must' for all with an interest in folk dance. There are parts for fairly accomplished recorder players and simple piano parts are also available. This book will also be of interest to the school music co-ordinator.

Adventures in Music Roy Bennett (1986), Longman.
This book encourages children to listen to music and provides a great deal of information about instruments and the occasions and places to which various pieces of music refer. This book will be valuable in the later years of the middle school, providing that the 'listening with enjoyment' aspect takes precedence over

the gathering of information.

Pitch In! The Oxford Percussion Course for Primary Schools, Jean Maughan, Stage 1 (1987), Stage 2 (1990).
Between them, these two books cover the whole of the primary age range. Both are listed here because, although the first book can be used from Y1, its application extends to Y5; the second of these books can be used from Y4 up to Y7 and beyond. The packages include teachers' books, wall charts and cassettes. Guitar chords and assistance with simple piano accompaniments are provided and there is discussion of a wide range of percussion instruments. There is emphasis on children reading music and these packs must be of value to the school music co-ordinator, though perhaps not for the non-specialist class teacher without help and advice.

Jazzylophone Kate Baxter, Schott & Co.
Music for upper juniors requiring teaching by music specialists who are prepared to let their hair down! An excellent book which, realistically speaking, requires practice before use in the classroom, when cross-curricular work can be attempted.

Sing at Christmas Anne Woolf-Skinner (1984), Schott & Co.
Three delightful carols which will be useful to music specialists with commitment to the use of pitched classroom instruments and recorders. The ability to play piano accompaniments is necessary. The children will need to be able to sing convincingly, occasionally in two parts, and this material will have to be carefully taught and rehearsed; it is well worth the effort.

Knucklebones Diana Thompson and Margaret Murray (1984), Schott & Co.
This book, for use with Y5 – Y7, contains excellent advice to teachers who have some specialist knowledge. Teaching suggestions about the use of the material, performances and audiences come before the actual music which consists of five

pieces for classroom performance. There is good advice also about related activities, teaching method, strategies and the solution of difficulties.

Strike it Rich (from 'Beaters' series) Colin Evans (1988), Schott & Co.
This book is for use with Y5 – Y7. It is great fun, but clearly for the specialist music teacher with a feeling for jazz.

Musicals

Novello has produced two musicals on an environmental theme which are published in association with the World Wide Fund for Nature, *Big Momma* and *The Bumblesnouts Save the World*, both by Debbie Campbell. They are not only performable as musicals. Individual songs are useful and a selection of them could be performed in a chosen method of presentation using dance and mime, children's artwork or in whatever way a school might decide.

The extent of a full blown musical would again be at the discretion of the school. If the music is to be played live, a reasonably accomplished pianist is required, though tapes which contain the piano accompaniment are available. On the tapes there are also versions which provide voice and piano and this would be very helpful in teaching and performing the works.

There are suggestions for the inclusion of unpitched percussion, though this is not essential. The songs are attractive and suitable for juniors and are by no means the sole property of the choir, but could simply be used as an opportunity for a 'jolly good sing'. Permission to perform the works must be obtained from the Performing Rights Society, but if no charge is to be made for entry, the performing fee is nominal.

Six Songs for St Andrews Sir Peter Maxwell Davies (1991), Longman.
This is playing and singing material of the highest quality for the junior school. A specialist music teacher who is a practised conductor will be required and the children will need to have a good grasp of the use of notation, though the instrumental parts are most cleverly and approachably written.

Pilgrimage Phillip and Jo Astle (1991), OUP.
This is a musical play about medieval times which includes many opportunities for music, dance and drama and a wealth of cross-curricular opportunities.

The book contains all that is needed to mount an impressive performance. The music has a true medieval flavour and is simply performed using the more commonly-found classroom instruments, but provision is made for the use of dulcimer, psaltery and violin which provide a more authentic sound. A tape is provided to assist in the learning of the music and work in dance.

Bartholomew Fair Phillip and Jo Astle (1991), OUP.
A most attractive publication of the same kind as *Pilgrimage*.

Instrumental books

Keyboard

Sing, Clap and Play Keyboard Garth and Heather Cox (1991), OUP.
There are *Sing, Clap and Play* books for other instruments, but this is a keyboard book for beginners which deals with the basic facilities on keyboards such as automatic rhythms, automatic chords and melodies played in differing tone qualities. There is an initial section on hand position and posture and it is thought that the smallest size instruments would probably be unsuitable for the purposes of this book. A child could very well work unattended at this material with occasional supervisory visits by a teacher. Teachers who are starting from scratch would also benefit from following the course.

Progression throughout the book is sensible and logical and the instructions are clear and well set out, though towards the end of the book some help will be required to supplement the section on written rhythm. A teacher who has some knowledge of the piano would easily be able to use this book with children. It is well produced and has a cheerful freshness about it which encourages listening skills instead of merely training children to reproduce what is on the page.

Start the Electronic Keyboard Nick Haines (1991), Longman.
There are two books in this series which demonstrate all the basic functions of the electronic keyboard. Very basic matters are covered in Book One, and by the time children have progressed to Book Two, they will have begun to hear the implications of the chords used so that the improvisation of accompaniments and 'busking' will be a likely outcome. The books will be useful to a teacher who can find time to provide some one-to-one teaching and certainly to a regular teacher of keyboard playing. The books deal exclusively with chords and the treble clef.

Keyboard Magic: And How to Achieve It John Hughes (1985), A & C Black.
This book could be very useful to a teacher who wanted to be able to use the keyboard but had not previously played the piano. After some practice it would enable a teacher to encourage children who were working on a child-orientated book, as it covers basic keyboard skills and explains the various effects found upon these instruments. It also contains a very useful index.

Recorder

Enjoy the Recorder: Descant Tutor (Book One) Brian Bonsor (1981), Schott & Co.
Enjoy the Recorder is an excellent book for the teacher who wishes to teach the instrument in a serious, committed and enjoyable way. It maintains a good balance between progressive and playable tunes, technique and teaching points. It provides a complete course and the teacher's book includes piano accompaniments.

From Descant to Treble (from 'Beaters' series) Brian Bonsor (1985), Schott & Co.
From Descant to Treble enables competent descant players to transfer to the treble instrument. It does not deal with the musical knowledge or technique since that is assumed to have been already covered. It is most useful although more pieces for descant/treble ensemble could have been included. Many recorder books are cheaper but few can be as good.

Play Time Stages 1 – 6 Margo Fagan (1973 – 1984), Longman.
A useful set of books catering, in the early stages, for young children. The teacher's book provides help for those with little or no experience in teaching the recorder, which is a good thing since the actual children's books leave a number of matters of technique and rhythmic notation to the teacher. These books are presented in a friendly format and should be considered when looking for a complete course.

Play Now Margo Fagan (1989), Longman.
This is a more immediate introduction to the recorder for slightly older children.

Play Together! Margo Fagan (1984), Longman.
Most of the tunes in this collection are for two parts.

Guitar

Abracadabra Guitar! A Book for Beginners Hilary Bell (1980), A & C Black.
An excellent tutor for teachers who want to use the guitar in the classroom but who have little time for practice. The song examples are variously useable throughout the primary age range.

Choral speaking

Crocodile and Other Poems Ruth Pollock Hamm (1988), Schott and Co.
This is a collection of poems for choral speaking with unpitched accompaniment for use with Y3 – Y6. It is a valuable introduction to both choral speaking and composition using rhymes and classroom instruments.

Ethnic music

World of Music, Arts and Dance – a teaching pack available from 26, Waterloo Street, Clifton, Bristol BS8 4BT (0272 734068). Although this material is largely aimed at the secondary age range, it would be of interest to any teacher who wanted to learn more about African and Indonesian music.

Pop, Rock and Ethnic Music in School Graham Vulliamy and Ed Lee (Cambridge Educational).
This book provides a mass of interesting information and is more likely to suggest ideas for teachers of the junior age range, though it is mainly aimed at secondary schools. It contains a useful bibliography.

Oxford Topics in Music Series, OUP.
This is a useful series with such titles as 'The Steel Band', 'Jamaican Music' and 'Medieval Music'. 'Indian Music' is strongly recommended as an insight into Indian life and musical culture.

Schulwerk

Music for Children, based on work by Orff and Keetman, Schott & Co.
   Book 1: Music for Children (Pre-school/Reception) English Ed. (1958)
   Book 2: Music for Children (Y1 – 4) English Ed. (1959)
   Book 3: Music for Children (Y4 – 7) English Ed. (1963)
Music for Children is not a series which can be satisfactorily used without some knowledge of *Schulwerk*. The philosophy behind this title relates to the work of Carl Orff and his life-long consideration of music for children which is, in itself, a specialised study. To use it well one needs to be a devotee of the *Schulwerk* approach. It is not to be dipped in to, but should form a central part of a teacher's planning and has to be backed up with knowledge and a stock of good quality instruments.

Details of courses and addresses from which information can be obtained will be available at any good music shop. With proper assistance *Schulwerk – Music for Children* is not difficult to initiate and the rewards will come in relation to the effort that a teacher is prepared to invest in learning about the system. These rewards, for children and teacher alike, can be considerable.

Glossary

Accent
A stressed sound within a series of sounds.

Accompaniment
Any set of sounds in a composition which are heard in a supporting role while a solo is being played.

Anacrusis
An incomplete bar at the beginning of a piece.

Bar
A small section of music between two bar lines (vertical lines down the five lines of music). The number of beats in the bar is indicated by the time signature ($\frac{4}{4}$ $\frac{3}{4}$).

Bass
The lowest voice of the four-part choir. Used also to denote the part played by the deepest instrument in an ensemble.

Beat
The regular pulse of music.

Chime bar
A single note played with a beater. The bar itself is made of metal which is mounted on a tubular or box-like resonator. Though produced in sets, chime bars can be purchased separately.

Chord
Two or more notes played together as a distinct sound.

Chromatic (instrument or scale)
An instrument or scale which contains, in terms of the piano, both black and white notes. A chromatic instrument or scale produces all the semitones available to the western ear, eg C, C#, D, E♭, E, F, F#, G, G#, A, B♭, B.

Clash
Notes which, when sounded together, produce an uncomfortable sounding result.

Clef
A sign at the beginning of a line of music indicating the note names and pitch of the five lines, eg treble clef (𝄞), bass clef (𝄢).

Consonance
An effect of two notes played together producing a feeling of stability and concord.

Crescendo
Growing louder.

Crotchet
A black-headed note with a stem; equal to two quavers or half a minim.

Cumulative songs
Songs which retain words from previous verses and add lines as the song progresses (eg Ten green bottles, One man went to mow).

Decrescendo
Growing quieter.

Diatonic (instrument or scale)
An instrument which contains only, in terms of the piano, the white notes. A diatonic scale contains only the seven notes of the major scale.

Drone
A note or notes of fixed pitch that continues throughout a section of music.

Dynamics
Variations in volume in a piece of music.

Echo games
Listening and playing games in which a played rhythm or snatch of tune is repeated as if in an echo.

Flat (♭)
A sign to lower the pitch of a note one semitone.

Glockenspiel
An instrument with metal bars which are

struck by beaters to produce a bell-like sound.

Groaner (or growler)
A derisive term applied to children who have not learned to control their vocal chords.

Harmony
The practice of sounding notes together to produce an overall effect; particularly applicable to the heritage of European music.

Interval
The distance between the pitches of two notes.

Key
The name given to the group of notes which make up a note family which is named after the first note of the family scale (eg the key of C major).

Key signature
A number of sharps, flats or the absence of either which denote the key in which the music is written and the notes to be used.

Major
A kind of key or scale which is thought to produce a bright and cheerful effect by the 'larger' distance between the first and third notes (eg C to E).

Melody
A tuneful arrangement of notes.

Minim
The term used for a white-headed note with a stem; equal to two crotchets or half a semibreve.

Minor
A kind of key or scale producing a more troubled effect because of the 'smaller' distance between the first and third notes (eg C to E♭).

Non-standard notation
Any graphic means of conveying the composer's intention to the player(s).

Notation
Any method of writing down music.

Note
A single sound (or symbol denoting the sound) of designated pitch and/or duration.

Octave
An interval of eight notes (eg from C to C').

Ostinato
A melody repeated throughout all or part of a piece of music.

Pentatonic scale
The five-note scale which can be formed upon any note which employs the first, second, third, fifth and sixth notes of the diatonic scale.

Phrase
A fragment of music, part of a melody, which has little use on its own but is a component in the structural balance of the whole melody. It is often written under a 'phrase mark' which looks like a rising and falling curve.

Pitch
This refers to the highness or lowness of a given note (eg a high-pitched scream).

Pitched instruments
Instruments able to produce notes of different pitches as, for instance, the glockenspiel. The wood block is an 'unpitched' instrument.

Polyrhythms
A kind of composition in which different rhythms of varying lengths are played together which produces a constantly shifting and varied effect.

Quaver
The term used for a black-headed note with a stem and a tail (the tails of these

notes are often joined); equal to half a crotchet.

Raga
The melodic element in classical Indian music.

Reggae
A type of Afro-Caribbean music.

Rest
Silence that occurs in a piece of music; indicated by various symbols that denote the length of silence.

Scale
A set series of notes which vary in content according to musical cultural background. These are the notes available to a composer in basic compositions, the scale most familiar to Western European ears being the diatonic major scale (eg C, D, E, F, G, A, B, C').

Semibreve
The term used for a white-headed note without a stem; equal to four crotchets and two minims.

Semitone
A half tone; generally the smallest interval in Western music.

Sequence
A repeated pattern of notes at varying pitches or a classroom composition which starts with a single instrument playing an ostinato to which other instruments and voices are joined. The instruments drop out one by one leaving the original ostinato.

Sharp (#)
A sign to raise the pitch of a note one semitone.

Skeleton songs
Also known in USA as 'zipper' songs, skeleton songs have a basic framework within the song which allows words to be made up. The simplest require the addition of single words, for example, 'On Monday we went shopping and we bought some............etc'.

Soprano
The highest voice in a four-part choir (similar in pitch to 'treble' which is used exclusively with boy choristers). The term soprano is also used for the highest sounding member of a group of similar instruments, for example, glockenspiel, xylophone, saxophone. In some countries the descant recorder is referred to as the 'soprano recorder', although the sopranino recorder sounds higher.

Staff (or stave)
A set of five parallel lines on, above or below which notes are placed to denote pitch.

Tenor
The highest adult male voice in a four-part mixed-sex choir. The term describes a member of a family of instruments as does 'soprano' above.

Timbre
A term used to indicate the characteristic qualities of a sound (eg a high, tinkling triangle has a different timbre to a low, thudding drum).

Time signature
This looks like a fraction placed at the beginning of a piece of music, the numerator giving the number of beats in a bar and the denominator giving the duration of each beat.

Tone
The distance between two notes of two semitones (see semitone).

Tone deafness
A vague term used to describe persons who have difficulty singing in tune. It is totally misleading as no permanent disability exists, but only a lack of practice in controlling the muscles of the vocal cords in relation to the pitch of a sounded

note. Disphonia is a medical condition which is rarely encountered but can be reasonably described as being 'tone deafness'. It occurs in less than two in a million.

Tonic sol-fa
A method of writing down vocal music or transmitting the required note by hand signs which enables singers to read and learn their music more easily than by having to learn staff notation. It is less widely seen nowadays but still has enthusiastic devotees and strong support from the Curwen Institute who have developed interesting uses in class and with instrumental pupils. The 'doh, re, mi, fa, soh, la, ti, doh' words are well known.

Word rhythms
A method of remembering rhythms to be played which uses the natural rhythms of words.

Xylophone
A pitched percussion instrument with bars made of wood which are struck with wooden or felt-headed beaters. A variety of types are available from the full orchestral instrument to the smallest classroom model.

Acknowledgements

The author and publishers wish to thank the following for their assistance, help and support:

Jeanette Coldham, Headteacher, Lee Common First School, Great Missenden, Buckinghamshire.

John Crofts, Headteacher, Turves Green Junior and Infant School, Birmingham.

Cliff Sage, Headteacher, St Stephens First School, Redditch, Worcestershire.

Geoff Bailey, Headteacher, Sidemoor First School, Bromsgrove, Worcestershire.

Roger Rippon, Headteacher, Pebworth First School, Worcestershire.

David Vincent, Headteacher, Cherry Orchard School, Worcester.

Steve Hutchinson.

John Thornton.

Barbara Stedeford.

Rehka Ladwa.

Helen Moulton, The Martineau Teachers Centre, Birmingham.

Peter Morrell and the staff of Coten End First and Middle School, Warwick.

...... and several children.